Orange, Black and Grey

Orange, Black and Grey

Mark Raines

Copyright © 2010 by Mark Raines.

Library of Congress Control Number: 2009911673
ISBN: Hardcover 978-1-4415-9596-6
Softcover 978-1-4415-9595-9

All rights reserved. No part of this book may be reproduced or transmitted in any form or by any means, electronic or mechanical, including photocopying, recording, or by any information storage and retrieval system, without permission in writing from the copyright owner.

This book was printed in the United States of America.

To order additional copies of this book, contact:
Xlibris Corporation
1-888-795-4274
www.Xlibris.com
Orders@Xlibris.com
68045

Be yourself, everyone else is already taken.

—Oscar Wilde

1

In plain view with the top three buttons unfastened, the perspiration on Alison's chest was a glistening indication of just how stifling it was. The air was decidedly oppressive in Baltimore that night, but in this off-the-beaten-path saloon, it must have been at least doubly so.

I glanced to my left where a handwritten note was adhered to a clear glass jar. "Donate to help a good friend recover from a cycling accident" was the plea. Without thought, I folded two one-dollar bills and inserted them through the man-made opening on the lid. In they went, their path abruptly halted by the curious amount of nickels lining the bottom.

"Another beer?" she asked. "Please," I replied while she bent over at a nearby cooler and reached for what was once the top-selling local brew but was nowadays enjoyed sparingly—and only then to mockingly enjoy what your parents and grandparents had in what, to all, seemed like halcyon days during which life was so much easier or, at least, simpler.

My own reason, however, for selecting this beer, one that could never hope to realize even modest popularity again, was hardcore faith. No, check that, I guess you could term it blind faith—or at least steadfast devotion. This poor girl. So conditioned was she that despite enduring the worst of the heat and discomfort, she remained genuine in her communication, her duties, and her smile.

There were, at the very least, about fifty other places I could have been that night—each of them offering an inviting facade and amenities foreign to my current location. But Charles Street was where I absolutely had to be. Not because of the one-dollar cans of a brand whose cult following was limited almost exclusively to those who represented by apparel, and nothing more. No, I had long since become addicted and resultantly, lost—first to the Orioles—and by now, to the world that was Baltimore. This particular venue was one I had discovered quite by accident. Attracted by its hideaway traits—a downstairs entrance and dimly lit room—I had since come to struggle with the enveloping humidity and raucous bantering that was altogether contradictory to any rendezvous with such an inviting front. Still, this is where I had made a calculated decision to drink on this Saturday. I didn't feel like being anywhere else. Least of all, where Bostonians were bound to be.

The Orioles struggled that night as they had for eleven straight years at this point. Manny Ramirez had launched career home run No. 500 off Chad Bradford. A highly unlikely round-tripper victim, the side-arming Bradford was hardly safe—none of the Orioles were—from the wrath of American League opponents, despite what his numbers and ground ball-inducing tendencies suggested.

The loss did not sit well. It was not for my fear of abandonment—I came to realize long ago that loyalty and civic pride are fleeting, indeed. My lone solace came in the fact that as Ramirez delivered his historic clout, I was protected in the bowels of Camden Yards while I dressed my Esskay hot dog.

The origin of this unconditional love is at times, cloudy, though specific telltale occasions—or thoughts thereof—only deepen an obsession that has long since spun out of control, unchecked, at times linked directly to acts of love, kindness, and giving and still on other dark afternoons/nights, decidedly selfish deeds.

It's difficult to put anything before Baltimore.

2

Spring 1975 arrived. A late bloomer at ten, I made my very first efforts on the baseball diamond. Other kids in my neighborhood—and it seemed like there were millions in Beverly, on Chicago's South Side—had begun playing at six, seven, and most definitely by eight.

I cannot explain my delay, but I can safely recall beginning a baseball card collection as the start to something that has reached heights I never intended to realize.

The opener neared, and jerseys (well, T-shirts) were distributed. I held my own up: KENNEDY PARK arched in white appliqué across the chest, and 15 screened in like fashion on the back.

"Who's number 15 on the Orioles?" I asked.

"I don't know, probably some shine," my coach replied.

I mention this not to cite the racial intolerance of that era and region but only to pinpoint that this is definitively my absolute earliest recollection of interest in the Orioles. Additionally, for anyone old enough to remember 1975, you'll readily agree that interest in Major League teams from other cities was hardly the norm. It's not that this was discouraged, but it simply wasn't an issue—for a number of reasons. The media coverage, for one, was not conducive to following a team that, in the Orioles' case, was 714 miles southeast. No cable or satellite television, no Internet, no Orioles coverage. As for apparel, I was limited to a replica cap that I could purchase only at Comiskey Park.

It's a safe bet that the black, orange, and white color scheme (introduced that year, as it had been black and orange only in previous seasons) and the cartoon bird were what wrested my impressionable ten-year-old eyes and mind.

Later that summer, I recall with certainty my first-ever live Orioles game. At Chicago's Comiskey Park, I watched as Baltimore fell to a ninth-inning rally that was fueled by a two-run homer off the bat of Brian Downing. I remember little else regarding that day (I'm certain it was an afternoon game), but games in the years that followed have stuck in my mind as though they were played two hours ago.

Again, that is my earliest semblance of loyalty to Baltimore, and while an introductory ninth-inning loss isn't typically the manner in which a ten-year-old is prompted to cling to what becomes a lifelong marriage, less-than-savory occurrences most definitely shaped my view that, sight unseen, Baltimore had to be a better place than the one I was in.

Directly across the street from my house was Mount Olivet Cemetery. As I grew up, a vacant strip (all grass) of four blocks in length and about two hundred feet in width was property of the cemetery but unoccupied by any plots. This was our baseball paradise. Home plate (an actual wooden example that my older brother had taken from somewhere) was installed about forty yards due east of Al Capone's modest (by gangster standards) tombstone. There were only three left-handed hitters among our group of about fifteen to twenty regulars: my younger brother, Dano Joyce, and Mouse Ryan. They were among the youngest, so it worked perfectly. They each hit about three or four home runs (over a freshly erected fence) before we all outgrew the place and moved elsewhere.

My older brother was king of the long ball—or so he liked to repeatedly claim. Actually, if records were to exist, he probably *was* the most proficient long ball hitter; but his incessant bragging invariably forced us all to talk of the power of other neighborhood kids.

And what made it worse was his insistence on perfecting his home run prowess—like going to the driving range, except the bucket of balls had to be delivered (and chased down) by me and my younger brother. To top it off, only he got to bat—for as long as he wanted—and when he was done, we all were done.

On one Saturday, I was the pitcher, positioned directly in line with this bully from whom there was to be no escape. He took aim for 115th Street as none of us thought to position the pitcher (that was me) at an angle so the batter could pull the ball. Shortly into the session, it happened: he hit a screaming line drive straight at me. It hit me square on the shin and caromed some thirty feet. Such were the hazards of being the younger brother (but not the baby brother) of an adolescent with a father complex.

And mine was no tale of woe. Contrarily, I had a magical childhood, playing baseball in marathon sessions until finally, I stood there as part of an actual team, holding my minor league Cubs T-shirt and examining the number on the back.

Turns out, "15" belonged to sparingly used outfielder Royle Stillman.

3

The interstate highways become more comfortable as you get farther from Chicago and closer to Baltimore. The airport is cleaner in Baltimore. Green lights last longer in Baltimore. These are not biased opinions, only facts as I know them. People with far greater political insight than I have, on several occasions, offered detailed explanation for the first of these comparisons. In short, the raw materials used in the construction of Illinois expressways are designed to fail. Hence, certain companies bid for the "new" projects, and revenue comes their way. Shunned is the rock-solid road that will withstand the elements.

A novice enthusiast at ten, eleven, twelve, I could only imagine what Baltimore was like. Shortly thereafter, I learned. For whatever reason, I attended no Orioles games in 1976, the last calendar year in which I did not see the Orioles live. Oh, I went to a few games with my older brother (I recall seeing a White Sox-Twins game). These were welcome experiences not realized via the Interlake-sponsored Perfect Attendance prizes I had won through my progress in grade school. I had begun to play halfway decent that summer, too, and started to really understand the game. I guess comprehensive understanding of anything is simultaneously a blessing and a curse.

Armed with diamond smarts and the knowledge of Major League combatants, I made my heartfelt choice—my first and, positively, my most significant—of an "opponent" to side with in September 1977. Saturday night, Orioles at White Sox. The Birds were felled, 6-3—despite an Al Bumbry home run. I distinctly recall three things that night. First, during batting practice,

Lee May hit the hardest ball not only that I ever saw, but I will also bet a sizeable amount that when we meet our maker, each of us can ask, "Lord, what was the hardest ball ever hit?" The reply will be, "My son, it was on an early September Saturday in 1977. On that night, Alabama-born Lee May hit a scorching line drive that not only cleared the wall but also hit the frickin' brick facade at the very back of the lower-deck bleachers—on a fly, I might add."

Lastly, I remember Johnny Rivers' "Slow Dancin'" playing on the radio on the way home in the car. Between May's and Rivers' hits, I remember feeling wronged (as has been the case after every setback since) and questioning how the Orioles could have lost.

4

Here I sit in a Charles Street saloon some thirty-one years later, and now, the losses are frequent. Some are devastating, some I see coming a mile down the pike. I can only wait patiently now. And while I do, I retain, somehow, the same conviction I had in the fall of 1977: how can the Orioles lose a game? This is a proud, fundamentally sound franchise. Fans everywhere will soon see that Baltimore is too good to be held down for more than a day or two.

I was a year old when a twenty-year-old rookie named Jim Palmer bested Sandy Koufax in the latter's last-ever outing (and decision). At four, five, and six, I sat idly in front of a record player while the Orioles won an aggregate 318 regular-season games (a three-year record among American League teams), three pennants, and a World Series title. At eight and nine, I remained a child recluse as the Orioles pitched their way (it was always pitching in Baltimore) to two more division titles.

In '75, I discovered baseball. So did the Boston Red Sox. The following year, I was hooked on baseball—as the New York Yankees returned to prominence. So as I declared an allegiance to the Orioles in 1977, they were a team stripped of free agents, destined for the lower ranks. Still, after the aforementioned setback at Comiskey Park, Baltimore remained in the thick of the AL East race. I followed, for the first time, on a daily basis. The best source at that time was the *Chicago Tribune* sports scoreboard line. A call to 222-1234 got me a recorded message of that day's baseball finals. No partial scores, only finals. But still, this was amazing technology! It was actually possible to pick up a phone and learn what happened at Memorial Stadium. I was in. Additionally, local news stations listed all of the out-of-town scores immediately following the highlights for the local teams.

I shan't forget the end to the 1977 Oriole hopes. Channel 5, WMAQ (NBC affiliate), the screen behind the sports desk read: BOSOX IN, ORIOLES OUT. And after a subsequent rainout, the two finished deadlocked for second, both having won ninety-seven games.

From that day on, I vowed to let nothing get between the Orioles and the World Series. As a fan, you somehow assume that your very presence—be it at the actual game or via broadcast—actually has something to do with the result. I am most certain that I am not alone in this belief. The further you are removed from the matter (specifically, in the depths of the off-season), the more ridiculous these thoughts of control seem. Nearly thirty years later, I can vividly recount the later stages of an August 26, 1979, twin bill against the White Sox.

There I was, alone in a seat down the right field line in front of the Oriole bullpen. As the White Sox threatened to author a win of the walk-off variety, the situation was potentially horrific on two fronts: (1) the obvious, the chance that the Orioles might lose, and (2) the fact that the next morning was to be my first day of high school. Surely my mother knew exactly where I was and also knew that, in addition to eight hours of baseball, a commute of at least an hour awaited me on public transportation westbound down Thirty-fifth Street and then southbound down Western Avenue from Thirty-fifth all the way to 108th. So I buried my face in my hands, believing that if I was not looking, it wouldn't happen.

And it didn't happen.

Instead, the Orioles completed a sweep on the strength of an extra-inning home run by Gary Roenicke. Today, I know full well that my actions had nothing to do with the outcome of that game. Nor has my attendance at any of hundreds of battles. Yet with each new game day, so many actions are calculated for the sole purpose of playing a hand in an Orioles triumph—from what socks I wear to which teeth I floss first to which writing utensil I use on my scorecard. Again, I have significant doubt that these rituals play any part other than to tax my everyday thought process. But until I understand that my life could be so much simpler—with no negative consequences to the Baltimore Orioles—I am to repeat these self-inspired actions. I fret not, however, as I know I'm not alone in such behavior. Perhaps more possessed by superstition, yes. But definitely not alone. While these actions went unannounced, my allegiance did not. As I witnessed a frantic surge that nearly made division champions of an overwhelming underdog installment in 1977, I was ready and willing to show undying support and spread the Oriole word like an evangelist spewing forth faith-based truths to all who would or would not listen.

And my truths were sacred.

5

Meticulous in alphabetizing every letter ever mailed to me, I find focus in these things (and in precious little else, it seems), knowing full well how much quicker it is to find a postcard filed under *M* and, one day, display it to former college buddy Tim Marley—he of great wit and with the pot-smoking prowess I made sure not to acquire. For starters, it allows for a methodic sorting—say, once every two years—in which I find little regret in telling myself (although not very often) that I no longer need this person's correspondence.

Some things lose their luster and, thus, their value.

Picking and choosing which of these messages have heartfelt, comical, or sentimental content worth retaining allows for an exact inventory of "friends"—including those with whom future contact is no longer even remotely possible. I cannot, however, recall the precise number of trips I've made from Chicago to Baltimore in the past twenty years. I do know for certain that all but one have been via airplane. And I do admit (or want to think, anyway) that I have become keenly more aware of my surroundings with each of these sojourns.

Very early in this endeavor, I recognized that my purpose was to sequentially piece together my experiences to discover how things fell into place or, probably more accurately, how they lack definitive ties of any sort, leaving me further in the dark in regard to a purpose or inspiration for it all.

Save for actual events to which I was a witness, I ask, what do I divulge to the person that does not share my passion? Do I describe my boundless excitement at the mere sight or sound of certain things? Nobody wants to be told what to love. When subject to browbeating of that intention, the adverse effect will take shape close to 100 percent of the time.

Baltimore has long been dubbed the "Charm City." I shall attempt to convey the irresistible attraction on that front. The key element here, of course, is the fact that "charm" is open to interpretation—especially in Baltimore's case. Every region has its quirks and characteristics. Each large metropolis, too, has traits and folklore that separate it from the rest.

While it certainly cannot fall into any genre, the following is my most accurate depiction of Baltimore in words:

I recall a recent night in a Baltimore saloon. As I awaited the scores on the ESPN ticker, I noticed the artful arrangement of bobblehead dolls on a mantle beside the television. There, I eyed a Brian Roberts (and recalled its "late" arrival as the manufacturer had mistakenly crafted the Roberts doll as a black player); Ravens' wideout Mark Clayton, Cal Ripken, Nick Markakis (a unique rendition of a slugger in a fielding pose—and appropriately); and two more whose pairing could only be subject to head-nodding approval locally and cries of blasphemy elsewhere. The two I speak of were Melvin Mora in a celebratory hand-slapping pose (a postgame ritual that he and Roberts undertook) and, on the receiving end of Mora's high five, none other than Jesus Christ, dwarfed by the more heroic (at least in this nativity scene of sorts) Mora. While putting your third baseman on an echelon right beside God is beyond reproach in perhaps any other town, in Baltimore, it comes down a simple choice: which of our heroes, from winning teams or not, goes toe-to-toe with Christ?

If not Mora, then Ripken or Ray Lewis.

This is Baltimore and, with it, Baltimore's infinite appeal. This is the city to which I must advance. It has not been easy. Nor is it going to get any easier. But I cannot lose sight of this humid, vagabond-infested metropolis as my final destination. The place I'll lie down to sleep every night.

And soon enough, I regress to the thoughts of an evolving fixation.

6

With the seeds of obsession sewn, 1978 introduced me to what is arguably any baseball fan's most intense passion: Opening Day. True, the vast majority clings to hopes for a week, maybe two—maybe less—but on that first Monday afternoon (in most instances), we all vow, with certainty, that this is the year. We're all just as good as or better than everyone else.

I was at the ready in 1978, my ears glued to 620 on the AM dial for the wry wit of WTMJ fixture Bob Uecker. And I happened to be fortunate that I had that much access to the opener as my broadcast feeds were limited to games against Milwaukee, Cleveland (three-W-E with Herb Score), Detroit (take your pick: WJR or WKZO, Kalamazoo), an occasional Minnesota Twins game, and on a really clear night, WBAP, Texas.

The very thought of it all prompts the question: is today's fan a little spoiled? Absolutely not. Funny, but I honestly would not trade those nights of fuzzy reception for complete live television coverage. Not a chance. Sure, I watch television broadcasts of games now, have for some time. But it's a simple truth that when limited to oral descriptions of an event, you're going to soak up and remember far more than you would had you experienced the audio-visual alternative. Positively. Via theater of the mind, I fell in love with a small market team that, when I was able to see it live, I identified with and appreciated even more. These were my Baltimore Orioles. And while their firm grip on absolute supremacy in the American League had somewhat loosened in recent seasons, it was about to become vicelike once again.

For just more than thirty years now, the American League East division has perennially been baseball's toughest—its players, mentors, and prospects trumping those in any other circuit. By all accounts, 1978 marked the start of this "dynasty," for lack of a more accurate term. Doing combat were the two-time defending league champion Yankees, the Red Sox, the Orioles—who had silenced all doubters with ninety-seven wins despite losing Reggie Jackson and twenty-game winner Wayne Garland. And as the Birds were to find out quickly, the Milwaukee Brewers began to flex their muscles.

Hindsight tells us that Baltimore could ill afford any tailspins that year, and that's precisely what the Orioles endured immediately, losing their first five contests by blowout margins. The Red Sox sprung from the gate and won at a torrid pace for nearly four months. The Yanks, of course, surged furiously to catch and pass their hated rivals, winning the division in a one-game playoff. Milwaukee, meanwhile, never really faded, not completely, anyway, and finished a respectable third. Lost in the shuffle were the Orioles.

They weren't lost in my shuffle, however. Contrarily, this team was right where I wanted it to be. Already buried in the standings, Baltimore showed all I wanted to see. In summary, the Orioles' performance (albeit a fourth-place showing) teased—and hooked—me. If ever a middle-of-the-pack finish could further entice a potential fan to commit to a lifetime of tickets, extra innings, winning streaks, losing streaks, arguments, and all things inherent to supporting any team, the 1978 Baltimore Orioles' effort was precisely that.

Left in the dust by the front-running BoSox—and ultimately, by the New York Yankees as well—the Orioles authored a thirteen-game winning streak that, to me, was not unlike a shot of heroin. I was somewhat addicted just prior to that lengthy run of success. For one, I recall a trip to Comiskey Park where I saw the White Sox do battle with the Angels. More accurately, I will say that my *brothers and cousins* witnessed that event. My own eyes were glued to the auxiliary scoreboard on the facade of the upper deck. In bright bulbs shaped into numerals, the very deliberate and unwanted verdict revealed that the Orioles lost to Detroit. I do not recall the score, nor do I remember the home and visiting teams. The reason it stuck with me is that it was the Birds' final setback before that thirteen-game winning streak got underway. Details of that were, from the few nuggets that come to mind, nothing short of glorious. I know the bulk of it was realized on a West Coast trip to Oakland, Seattle, and Anaheim. As was the case at the White Sox-Angels contest just days prior, I chose not to partake in the activities my immediate family members were enjoying. Vacationing at a cottage on a beach in Michigan, I was all too aware of what the Orioles were doing, so AM radio broadcasts—not sand castles and swimming—comprised the fare on my "vacation." All a matter of choice.

I recall reports that Oakland (a god-awful team at that juncture) was unveiling an eighteen-year-old starter named Mike Morgan. We beat him. What finally stopped Baltimore was what, coincidentally, was to stop the Orioles in their final game at hallowed Memorial Stadium. Downing the O's some thirteen seasons apart, Frank Tanana laid his first "bookend," halting the winning streak at thirteen games—as I took in *Damien: Omen II* at a local theater.

You always remember what you were doing when significant things take place. Always.

7

Upon observing a map of the city of Baltimore, you'll find that it is shaped almost exactly like the state of Nevada. Put the images side by side, however, and I will immediately point out which one is Baltimore: it's the one with the chewed-up lower corner. That corner, incidentally, represents the shores of the Chesapeake Bay—the Inner Harbor. Who wouldn't want to take a bite of such a delectable portion?

As my unchecked interest had grown, it was only a matter of time before I had to visit the city of Baltimore. A few months into the 1978 season, I spearheaded a charge to realize this journey. Having recruited my mother to organize the entire project, I had a mid-August date with the Orioles and New York Yankees. While double digits separated the Yankees (and the Red Sox) from Baltimore, I honestly thought it was no big obstacle. I was ultimately wrong, of course; but in Baltimore for the first time in my life, I could be hindered by no deficit whatsoever. My expectations—exceedingly high as they were—were met and surpassed. This was a whole new world. Everything I needed. My inaugural Orioles home game was a Saturday afternoon affair. To this very day, I cannot remember being as hot as I was that day. The temperature had to be over a hundred degrees, and to make it absolutely oppressive, the humidity was about 1,000 percent. Scott McGregor mowed down the Yanks (as he did to just about every opponent back then) with relative ease, topping out at about eighty miles per hour while the batters anticipated another chance, one by one, until there were suddenly no more chances. Staked to a 3-0 lead after six innings, McGregor was touched for five runs in the top of the seventh.

And then, the sky opened up.

As definitive as the heat had been, so was this rainstorm. To me, it looked like about twenty bad storms occurring all at the same time. And this downpour had staying power. So much so that about two hours later, the umpiring crew called the game. Unlike the current rule, the rainout definition in 1978 went as follows: if the visiting team had batted at least five innings, the game was official. Additionally, once an official game was halted, you reverted back to the last completed inning to arrive at your final score. Thus, the Yankees had a 5-3 advantage but had assumed their lead after seven at bats while the Orioles were only afforded six.

In summary, I witnessed a 3-0 shutout. Justifiably, that scare I endured turned out to be no more than a frightening storm, if you will.

Did I find you or did you find me?

—Shawn Colvin

8

Our strongest and most meaningful relationships begin by chance. Almost always.

We can (and often do) single out a potential partner and set out to court that person. I will keep appearing where she appears, formally meet her, ask her out; and from there, we will live happily into old age.

But that's not how it happens, is it? No, our real loves, soul mates, if you will (not those with celestial properties we only see from afar), are met via chance.

I was driving home one afternoon in late January 2003. Going south on Harlem Avenue at around 103rd Street, I stopped as the light turned red. Now had that light stayed green, I'd have kept going. I would not have been stopped alongside a strip mall. I would not have told myself to turn into that strip mall.

And I would not have taken home what was to be my roommate for nearly three years.

It was all chance. A simple red light.

I turned into the strip mall and walked into the pet store. There she was, the fattest goldfish I had ever seen. "I'll take that one," I told the store owner. Along with my new aquatic friend, I purchased a sizable glass bowl and some flakes—my pal's breakfast and dinner, six flakes per serving.

Shortly after bringing my fish home, I came upon an Orioles keychain with the name Brenda on it. This was my fish's name: "Brenda." I've never been big on pets. I don't see their purpose. You can't talk to them; all you can do is feed them and clean up after them. I know that millions of dog owners will claim that their pets have distinct personalities. I don't buy it. Did Brenda have a personality? I don't think so. She was crazy about the flakes, though. I do know that. She was stationed on a dresser next to my bed. When I went to bed each night, I'd put six flakes in her bowl, hit the light, and lie down to *crunch, crunch, crunch* in rapid fashion.

I took good care of Brenda. I believe she got an eye infection once. It looked painful. All I could guess was that it was caused by soap residue I hadn't completely rinsed off the bowl (that fish always had undoubtedly the cleanest bowl in the Northern Hemisphere—I made certain of that). The bulge in her eye went down almost immediately, and (I assume) we both felt a lot better.

I'm not sure of the life expectancy of a goldfish, but Brenda must have exceeded those. She lived (with me) for close to three years. That has to be some kind of record, no? In December 2005, I noticed that she wasn't so eager to eat. I knew that the end was near when I returned from work two days consecutively and found leftover flakes still in her bowl. On December 5, 2005, Brenda checked out. There she was, floating, motionless. I knew it was coming. I wasn't sad or distraught like many pet owners. The situation really didn't warrant any emotions.

I did realize, however, that this fish was there for a ride of nearly three years. Whether caring for her made a difference in my life or not, I did it as part of a daily routine. For those two-plus years, Brenda was as much a fixture at my place as the black walls and the Orioles-themed decor.

So I acted accordingly.

I cleaned her bowl. I still have it—along with whatever flakes remained. I rinsed Brenda and put her into a ziplock bag and put it in the freezer. Twenty days later, I woke up, pulled the bag out of the freezer, and carried it to Midway Airport. There, I boarded a Christmas morning flight to Baltimore. The Ravens were playing that night.

Upon arriving, I caught a Light Rail train to downtown Baltimore; and before checking into my hotel, I walked to the Inner Harbor and gave Brenda the proper burial.

After someone dies in the movies, they'll usually show a funeral on a cold, dark day—whether those were actually the conditions that day or not. On the day I buried Brenda to sea, it was unusually warm, about sixty-five degrees, and raining. On Christmas Day.

9

There's always going to be a prettier girl. The first is significant because the feeling is unprecedented. Has there been anyone more important than Laura Withington from my 1970 kindergarten class? I doubt it. I think I was a stalker at five. I mean, I still know exactly where she lived; and unlike five-year-old boys who pick on or berate their female contemporaries as a dead giveaway that they have an unbridled crush on them, I think I was somehow probably more interested in going down on my crushes—at age five. I should have known then that I'd have a problem with obsession.

Prettier girls, of course, have come and gone. So have better-tasting pizzas, funnier stand-up acts, and more comfortable pillows.

A more scenic and awe-inspiring edifice than Memorial Stadium, however, has not been encountered. Not by me. This is not to say that Camden Yards isn't gorgeous. Because it is. Perfect location, beautiful flag court, majestic scoreboard (especially when viewed from Eutaw Street as you enter the venue).

But smack in the middle of the Waverly neighborhood, there stood a magnificent structure I was to adore without respite. In my ensuing visits to this Thirty-third Street palace, I recall deboarding the No. 8 bus on Greenmount Avenue, walking to Memorial Stadium, and then circling the entire facility before choosing an entrance. I loved the sacred, monument-like light towers. I was equally inspired by the greenery beyond the outfield walls. And finally, the turnstiles reminded me that every time I presented my ticket to an usher in his bright orange suit coat, I was about to see a well-oiled machine that—while not nearly as celebrated as so many other rosters—was unrivaled in terms of quality pitching, airtight defense, and team-taught strategy that shaped each player from Bluefield to Charlotte to Rochester and, ultimately, here on Thirty-third and Ellerslie.

It wasn't until that first Baltimore experience that I realized that I was perhaps a bit more enthusiastic than even the locals. Actually, I know that full well in retrospect, but at the time, I could not grasp any such concept. In the hotel room at the Cross Keys Inn, I recall a local game show. The reason I can pinpoint it as being local (unusual for a game show, no?) was the host's comments. As he and the contestant got acquainted, the subject of the Orioles came up. From there, I remember the host proclaiming that this was kind of "an up-and-down season" as he teetered around his free hand.

How could he make such a statement? Was he not watching the same team I was? I still do not believe that my own assessment was lofty. Sure, that team was to finish in fourth place, but ninety wins is ninety wins; and that pretty much marked the beginning of American League East dominance that, to this day, hasn't waned in the least.

It was time to let the world know about this team, this well-kept secret that I had—with unprecedented serendipity—stumbled upon. I was thirteen, and I was dead certain about a few things: I loved baseball, I could not or would not ever be able to play it without embarrassing myself, and I enjoyed writing. I had the perfect outlet in my eighth-grade English class: a daily journal entry on whatever subject I saw fit. Miss Belfuss was the teacher, and I inundated that poor woman with daily accounts of the Orioles and what they meant to the world. As the season approached the final weekend and my Birds had been mathematically eliminated (prayers to St. Jude and nightly rosary vigils *did* stave off the inevitable for a short while), I penned a poem. The entirety of it is forever lost to me, but it opened like this:

> The Baltimore Orioles hitting parade
> Will go to Detroit, where cars are made.

Aside from previewing the Orioles' meaningless final weekend series at Tiger Stadium, this literary gem told of the remarkable things to come. In this, my holy bible, the words of the prophet spilled forth without interruption.

And oh, what a soothsayer I was.

Kings and things to take by storm, as we go along our way.

—Steven Schwartz

10

The 1979 season shaped me more than did any other single event, lengthy trial or person's influence. It is for this reason that I will forever look back on it (often with clarity reserved for a week-old occurrence) with simultaneous fondness and angst.

In summary, while there will never be another Memorial Stadium, or any other since-razed structure, nor will there ever be another 1979 Baltimore Orioles.

It's not difficult to pinpoint the peak of my unconditional adoration of a franchise. By fourteen, I became decidedly familiar (albeit from better than seven hundred miles west). I gave my all in '79. And so did the Orioles.

While I cannot recall the specifics regarding the Birds' Las Vegas odds that spring, I am quite certain they were deemed as not only noncontenders but also as such with little or no chance to match New York, Boston, or Milwaukee—let alone any rivals from the AL Western division.

I was keenly more aware of the Orioles' prospectus, however. And that in itself is nothing to brag about. I made my prognostications more from fact than did Las Vegas, which, I'm assuming, based its forecast almost entirely on team personnel and recent results.

Opening Day marked not only the start of Baltimore's march to supremacy, but it also signaled my own invasion of the basement of our home on Chicago's South Side. In the corner, I constructed a replica of Memorial

Stadium, complete with artificial grass (from a local hobby store) and functioning floodlights. That was my office. The couch was my bed. I left only for school and, in the summer, for lob league baseball with a select few friends.

By mid-June, the Orioles had taken the sporting world completely by storm. I had expected it all along. On Friday, June 22, my mother dropped me off at my grandmother's house in nearby Oak Lawn. While the majority of fourteen-year-olds would have balked at such a destination, I always liked it there. And on this particular night, I had live Orioles action to accompany me via the feed from Detroit's WJR on the AM dial. Bottom of the ninth, two outs, and through the crackling reception, I heard Ernie Harwell tell me that Doug DeCinces had just hit a two-run homer to win it for Baltimore.

There I sat, on June 22, knowing full well that nobody was going to catch this team. Shortly thereafter, *Time* featured an image of Earl Weaver in the upper right-hand corner of its cover with accompanying text that read, "Baseball's Shocker: Orioles Up, Yankees Down."

Baseball may have been shocked, but I wasn't.

There wasn't much that didn't go right that summer. I won tickets on WLS to a Comiskey Park concert that featured the Beach Boys, Blondie, and Atlanta Rhythm Section. I liked them all—probably just because it was 1979. President Jimmy Carter was on the cover of the aforementioned *Time* magazine. Carter is, to this day, my favorite president. I don't know what he did, good or bad.

I only know that it was 1979, and he was our president.

Of course, there were cries from sportswriters and broadcasters. Reminders, if you will, of the amazing charge that the Yankees had staged just one summer prior as they erased a seemingly insurmountable deficit in catching—and passing—the Red Sox. But I wasn't concerned in the least of the Orioles faltering as Boston had. In fact, the lone distraction was of a business nature. That summer, renowned criminal attorney Edward Bennett Williams purchased the Orioles. As I learned of this via a newscast on Chicago's NBC affiliate, WMAQ, sportscaster John O'Reilly (I'll never forget that son of a bitch) read the teleprompter and proceeded to add, "You can bet that team will be in the Nation's Capital by 1980." News, John, no editorials. Besides, you were wrong, you ignorant bastard. Who are these people who think that their word is gospel?

August was upon us—the dog days that often separate contenders from pretenders. And it opened in tragic fashion as Yankee catcher Thurman Munson was killed in an aircraft crash as he practiced landing on a Yankees off day. There were, unbeknownst to many, two survivors from that crash, making it all the more heart-wrenching. The Orioles were scheduled to open a four-game series at Yankee Stadium the next night. Hearing suggestions that the Friday night opener be cancelled as the team mourned its fallen backstop, Munson's widow told the team to play, that Thurman would have wanted it that way.

For the Friday night contest, I was limited to updates from sports phone, which told me that the Orioles had a 1-0 lead on a John Lowenstein home run. That's all we needed, and that was the final score. Baltimore prevailed again the next night, too. The Yankees did come back to win both the Sunday game and the nationally televised Monday night battle, but Baltimore went to Milwaukee the following series, and again, I had an AM radio from which I could somehow control the outcome.

In one of those games with the Brewers, Steve Stone pitched a one-hitter, and the Orioles won, 2-1. More than ten years later, I ran into Stone on a ramp at Wrigley Field and asked him what his greatest performance was. He was very accommodating. He mentioned the 1980 All-Star Game in which he pitched three perfect innings but disqualified that as an exhibition and proceeded to explain the game against the Brewers with a "Charlie Moore solo home run being the only thing that rained on my parade."

We both remembered it. It was, after all, 1979.

There was, in my qualified opinion, nothing that was capable of derailing the Oriole Express that year. A Memorial Stadium-issued button said it best: "The Bird Will Fly."

Division title, American League Championship Series—neither even remotely posed a challenge. (Though I do recall the O's blowing a late lead to prevent what would have been a three-game sweep of the Angels—with Richard Nixon in attendance—further cementing my Carter favoritism.)

What I feared least of all was our World Series task against the Pirates.

And after the first four games—the last two of which were secured by the Orioles with stinging come-from-behind rallies—it was all but a done deal.

But the 7-1 loss in Game 5 did not sit well with me. Headed back home or not, the Orioles had suddenly stopped hitting. Sure enough, in Game 6, they were shutout. Then it came: Wednesday, October 17, 1979, far and away the most emotionally draining day of my life. As I boarded one, then a second, CTA bus on my fifty-minute commute to high school, I distinctly remember studying each and every passenger. Had they any idea what was simultaneously going on in Baltimore? Did they have a vested interest? Did they care one way or another who was going to emerge victorious that cold night?

Then I looked for indicators.

If anyone had any Pirate yellow or gold in their apparel, any of it, I subtly pointed an index finger in their direction and pulled my hand back—again, subtly—as if I was firing a pistol in the direction of one of their vital organs.

This is what it had come to. It was far too much for the heart and psyche of a fourteen-year-old to handle. It was for me, anyway.

As Rich Dauer strode to the plate in the third inning that night, I absolutely knew that a home run was going to be the outcome of the at-bat. Not an expected result, mind you, of a Dauer at-bat. Gut feeling confirmed—Orioles 1, Pirates 0.

History tells us, of course, what ensued: a Willie Stargell home run off Scott McGregor with two outs and a man aboard in the sixth. Pittsburgh tacked on two more in the top of the ninth to make it 4-1. I recall the Memorial

Stadium sound system playing the Beach Boys' "Don't Worry Baby" as yet another Oriole reliever was summoned to stop the bleeding. The club always played appropriately themed or titled songs. When a player went down with an apparent injury, on would come Carly Simon's "Haven't Got Time for the Pain." When the Orioles shelled an opposing starter and his manager made a second trip to the mound in the same inning (by rule, putting an official end to that pitcher's night), Johnny Paycheck's "Take This Job and Shove It" prompted laughs from anyone who made the not-so-subtle connection.

But despite the magic that had brought us to the ninth inning of Game 7 of that 1979 World Series, Brian Wilson's lyrics failed to sooth me. I did, indeed, worry.

I knew it was over, and it was. This was the best baseball team I had ever seen. Better than any club I had seen before and better than any team I've seen since. I was never as remotely distraught in my entire life, and despite subsequent events that suggest otherwise, I invite the return of any such heartbreak rather than relive what I endured that Wednesday night.

11

Despite what has been conveyed thus far, my heartfelt beliefs aren't entirely Pavlovian responses certain to promote all things Maryland. I'll be the first to offer what I insist to be the only true explanation of a certain phenomenon restricted to citizens in the 301 area code. There, near Silver Spring, Maryland, and the Washington, D.C. area, people receive notice (I assume via the United States post office) to make a trip to the Motor Vehicle Administration and pick up their driver's licenses. This occurs, as it does in other states, when the person reaches sixteen years of age.

The difference in the 301 area code, however, is that the aforementioned constitutes the entire procedure. In other words, they get a document and go trade it in for a driver's license. No driver's test—written or otherwise. Here's your license, now go get behind the wheel, and best of luck.

Now, I've never actually witnessed this, but I'm positive that is the way they do it in the 301 area code. Never, never, never have I been in traffic with people who are less capable of operating a motor vehicle. City traffic, expressways—doesn't matter. Actually, the latter roadways are more aggravating because if another vehicle is pulled off to the shoulder with—oh, take your pick—a flat tire, a traffic citation, these 301 area code people slow down and actually come to a complete stop and stare at what you could swear is a form of entertainment that knows no rivals in terms of excitement and originality.

No, leave me to the city limits of Baltimore, thank you. I needn't expand my horizons or befriend anyone outside Charm City proper.

12

My world in ruins—at fourteen—it was "Game 1" from that point forward. As I matured toward adulthood, I noticed that my peers did, as well. Do yourself a colossal favor: if you can arrange to avoid adulthood, by all means, do so. Like so many other situations in which growth is automatically deemed "progress," age and physical development, for the most part, represent the exact opposite.

Thursday, October 18 was a tough day. My first realization was that I had not been in some parallel universe the previous night. The Orioles were, in fact, felled and, come 1980, would have to knock off American League opponents one by one—again. And should they accomplish that arduous task, another best-of-five ALCS had to be conquered as did a World Series opponent.

And the school day began in Mr. Dyar's freshman Spanish class at St. Laurence High School. I wasn't from the neighborhood. I didn't know a single classmate (a standing of which I was sincerely glad), and logically, they didn't know me either. But there I was: the freshman who wore the Orioles jacket.

As I took my assigned seat for first period, it didn't take long. Ralph Georza, a rotund sort with a unibrow thing going on, took the first shot.

"Black and gold is where it's at, baby!"

His reference, of course, was to both the Pittsburgh Pirates' and our high school's team hues. Now this guy had never spoken to me before—nor was he to ever speak to me again. In other words, his lone objective was to remind me that Baltimore had lost, to remind me that I was going to have to think about it all winter, to remind me just how difficult it is to get as far as the Orioles had the night before, and to remind me that it might not happen again next year or in 1981 or 1982.

He knew exactly how cruel his statement was. He didn't give a shit about the Pirates. Truth be told, the areas from which we all hailed were almost exclusively American League in terms of fan base. I knew that then, I know it now. Until he saw me wearing an Orioles jacket, I doubt he even knew there was a World Series taking place.

More than twenty years later, I was working as a pari-mutuel teller at a Chicago offtrack betting parlor. One Saturday, I saw Ralph Georza in there, placing bets. He was the same. Loud, obnoxious. The only possible difference between Ralph Georza of October 18, 1979, and the Ralph Georza I saw twenty-plus years later was that the latter version was a little bit fatter. I will wager any takers that there is absolutely zero possibility that had this guy spotted me, he would've recognized me by face or name.

But I'll never forget that prick.

From the tone of his bellowing, his equine wager was probably a profitable one. I was then hoping he would approach my window to cash his ticket or, better yet, to make a last-minute wager on another race. I was set to feign unfamiliarity, reach for the power button beneath my machine, and inform him that the "system was rebooting."

This was, as I mentioned, better than twenty years removed from the cutting remark he made as a fourteen-year-old high school freshman. A possible debate in this situation might be one for me to grow up. As I stated earlier, growing up is not something in which I take interest. Nor is answering to anyone when I am in no way doing harm to anyone or anything. Finally, I don't care if three hundred years had elapsed since Ralph Georza's biting remark; he started it, and I'm not about to forget it.

He wasn't the only one. He was just the first. His "binding" of the Pirates and St. Laurence High School immediately pitted me against my own school. I wanted its athletic teams (which were pretty decent at that time) to lose in each and every arena. A year later, maybe two, I recall Mr. Kocher. Good guy (as were most of the mentors at my high school). I liked him, and he tolerated me. He was my homeroom teacher, and every Friday, he'd play this game called "Joe Predicto" in which each student would predict the final score of the upcoming weekend's St. Laurence football game. The closest to the accurate total was to be awarded additional points on a subsequent test score (incentive for handicapping, maybe, but a really bad lesson regarding learning). Each Friday, he'd walk to each desk, take the slip, and read the student's name and prediction.

"Witters, St. Laurence, 38; St. Rita, 16 . . . McClean, St. Laurence, 42; St. Rita, 7 . . . Plotke, St. Laurence, 28; St. Rita, 0 . . . Raines . . ."

He wouldn't read my prognosis. After the first two weeks, as a matter of fact, he crumbled my sheet and left it on the floor for me to pick up each Friday.

Not only did I pick the opposing team every week, but I called for scores the likes of 77-0, 85-0 (always a shutout).

The word was out. One time I was spit on, a shove here or there. Nothing major. I was never one to fight back, nor was I ever about to back down and change my stance on the Orioles or my opposition toward "their" hometown and its every element. And it wasn't all bad. I did make a few friends—including this kid Andy who started to wear an Orioles cap, himself. A proselyte, if you will. I was, by no means, recruiting. It wasn't about popularity or even being different. I just wanted the Orioles to win and to mind my own business—and for my classmates, fellow commuters, bus drivers, store clerks, and random passers-by to mind theirs, as well.

Anyway, as my grades were to ultimately indicate, St. Laurence High School was not my focus.

The Baltimore Orioles were.

Porgi, amor, qualche ristoro al mio duolo, a' miei sospir; o mi rendi il mio Tesoro, o mi lascia almen morir.

—Wolfgang Amadeus Mozart

13

The fall and winter months went by. United States hostages were taken into captivity in Iran. Disco, despite vehement opposition, was still pretty much the coolest music around. Daylight was brief.

And the hurt from the previous October did not subside. Not in the least. It was at this juncture that I probably came to realize (though I cannot remember for certain) that I was in this for the long haul. Forever. At home and at school, my obsession was no secret. Simultaneously, the Orioles' strengths were suddenly common knowledge, as well. As spring training arrived, my mother (paying no heed to spring training of course) planned a trip—the first of what was to become an annual excursion of sorts—to Miami, Florida. Only problem was that the trip was to extend shortly past the 1980 season opener, which happened to pit the Orioles against the Chicago White Sox in my South Side hometown.

She, of course, arranged for me to depart Florida early while my family stayed on so I could be home to attend the Orioles' opener. I'm not sure if I conveyed how grateful I was for her tolerance, her catering, her suppression of what I'm certain had to be aggravation over a son whose obsession had now translated to an inconvenience. I've told her since that I'm appreciative, not just for that but for the countless times that she and she alone was able to distinguish between selfish behavior and an addiction. Whatever disciplinary streak she may have had became transparent to my siblings and me at a very young age. It worked, though, because subconsciously knowing how lucky we were, we never acted as though we knew that her seldom threats were completely empty (which they were, every last one of them).

I can say in complete honesty that my mother was openly angry with me on one occasion. And it was for, ironically, something that I did not do.

My memory of the incident is vivid in spurts. I was somewhere around five or six years old, walking down Fairfield Avenue with my broken bicycle (I believe the chain came off). A mere three doors from my own home, I strode past the Bruss' house where Mr. Bruss was seated on his porch. The gist of what then happened consisted of him asking me if I wanted him to fix my bike and me (fearing that he might have to keep the bike or that it would never be repaired) refusing—politely.

What ensued is not at all hazy.

The daughter, Patti (two years my senior), walked down, knocked on our door, and informed my mother that I had been rude and swore at her father.

What the fuck?

I know what I was and wasn't capable of at that age, and I'm guaranteeing that I said nothing rude, whatever, to that bald-headed liar.

In all probability, my mother was having a bad day to begin with because she dismissed Patti Bruss, grabbed me by the arm, and led me up to the bathroom—with unprecedented anger and force. The bar of soap went into my mouth, and I was interrogated repeatedly, "What did you say to Mr. Bruss?!"

"I didn't say nothin'!" was all I could contend.

After what was probably about fifteen seconds (a long time with a bar of soap in your mouth), I reasoned to myself that I had better blurt out a swear word or this isn't going to stop.

Finally, "FUCK!" came out. Loud and clear. I figured that was a good-enough term to end on.

It ended, all right. With a deeper insertion of Ivory and a few sharp tugs of my hair.

I'm not even sure if she remembers that. It's damn near my favorite memory, if only for the fact that it was totally out of character for both of us: I was mild-mannered—certainly not a kid who would tell a would-be bicycle repairman to fuck off—and she was incredibly patient, understanding, and supportive (and none of those attributes to a fault).

In the end, it was a far less-trying ordeal than the 1979 World Series. At least then, I'm sure it wasn't a matter of days—maybe even hours—before I was back on my bicycle speeding past the Bruss' house (in both directions) without a second thought.

Getting back to the October spotlight, on the other hand, wasn't going to be nearly as easy.

14

I'm pretty certain I was allowed to go back to Chicago on my own that April. Such a minor detail is forever obscured by the actual flight from Miami to Chicago.

As if to send a message that he hadn't completely abandoned me, God arranged (there's absolutely no other explanation) that I flew back on the Orioles' chartered flight. They weren't all there, mind you. No Murray, Palmer, Roenicke, Lowenstein, Flanagan, or McGregor. But I met and had my picture taken with the likes of Earl Weaver, Tippy Martinez, Tim Stoddard, (the late) Pat Kelly, and Sammy Stewart—who has since fallen on times and circumstances far more taxing than any World Series loss.

I knew right then that this was as close as I would ever come to being an actual member of the team. Oh, I had taught myself to switch-hit—and even did it in organized games at the Senior League level. But I was never going to hit any breaking balls or anything faster than 60 mph.

In summary, I had the unique ability to strike out from either side of the plate.

The fleeting thought of donning a uniform and taking the field evaporated quickly. I needed *them* to get back on the field and get right to business. I wanted a repeat of the year before—minus the Hitchcock ending. Opening Day provided an auspicious start to fulfilling that wish: same result (win), same opponent (Chicago), same winning pitcher (Palmer), and same score (5-3). For the first time in months, I felt as though I wasn't wounded.

Frigid Chicago temperatures, however, coincided with frigid Oriole pitching and hitting for the remaining three games of the series—all of which we lost.

Confronted at Comiskey Park by another high school classmate (this one, Chuck Wills, slightly less of a jagoff than the earlier-mentioned teen), I listened to raves of how great the White Sox were. This I could deal with. For one, there was no finality. It was April for Chrissakes, and whether or not I was more mature than my peers, I was a thousand times more knowledgeable in regard to baseball. I knew my Orioles product. I knew their White Sox product. And I knew that by the All-Star break, we'd be on opposite ends of the spectrum.

And so we were.

15

I know all about ebb and flow. My cousin utters those very words when someone bitches about their luck during a night of poker. From what I've experienced, he's actually spot on. Ebb, flow, peaks, valleys—however you want to define it—every endeavor is going to be easy for some periods and near-impossible at other times.

Try explaining "ebb and flow" to teams and their fans in the American League East.

First and foremost, the Yankees have and always will have the capability to actually print as much currency as they desire and spend it on anyone they please. In recent seasons, as I down yet another Natty Boh and cringe at the reality of it, the Red Sox have elevated to a similar financial plateau.

In this, the age of eight-, nine-, ten-, eleven-, twelve-digit salaries (all in the Bronx, it seems), too many are quick to forget that back in 1980, the Orioles were geographically challenged. Specifically, winning one hundred regular-season games got them no more than some lovely parting gifts while the division-champion Yankees advanced to (and lost) the ALCS.

As for the race for the American League East title in 1980, the "rush" or "thrills" on any high-speed Six Flags roller coaster or Terror Tower (I'm told that one is appropriately named) pale in comparison to what transpired between the Orioles and Yankees during the edge-of-your-seat summer of 1980. For starters, the Orioles were as many as fourteen games out in mid-July. An incredible surge ensued, however, and by mid-August, Baltimore was within sniffing distance of the lead.

Every game was of the must-win variety. My mother took my brother, a close friend, and me up to Milwaukee one weekend; and we attended a Brewers-Indians game (inconsequential, to be sure, but American League East entertainment, nonetheless). Desperate for every update, my eyes were glued to the auxiliary scoreboard for the length of the game. In the end, I was informed via those magical gold-colored bulbs that the Orioles had staged some late-inning heroics and defeated the Yankees (at Yankee Stadium, if I recall correctly). While my travel companions were enjoying County Stadium and, subsequently, the amenities at the Pfister Hotel, I was in my own heaven. The Indians happened to be staying at the Pfister and, later that night, I saw Rick Manning walking from the bar toward the lobby.

"Hey, Rick," I said, quite comfortably. "You know if you guys win tomorrow and the Blue Jays lose, you're not in last place anymore."

"Who gives a fuck," he deadpanned and kept right on walking.

Fully aware that a Major League contract doesn't prohibit one from saying "fuck," I had a very distinct interpretation of Rick Manning's response that night. I wasn't offended. Not at all. But I immediately thought to myself that his answer reflected his attitude. Analyzing further, I deduced that people like Manning, in large part, are the reason Cleveland hasn't won a World Series since 1948.

At the risk of sounding naive, I truly didn't think that any baseball-related comment would elicit such a response from an Oriole player. Not then. Man, 1980 was great.

There were two August nights on which the thing was ours for the taking. Out on the West Coast (as were the Yanks), the Orioles were within one-half game for a few days. In an incredible turn of events, we got some very unexpected help as the lowly Oakland A's beat the Yankees on two successive nights. But the Orioles, meanwhile, lost on the same nights to the just-as-lowly Seattle Mariners.

They never did take over first place—not even for a few seconds (which I believe was all they needed to do).

16

The first game, the glory of the late 1970s, the resultant fixation—they're all deep in the past now. But I cannot let go any easier today than I could have five years ago. And the years seem to blend now. With each trip back to Baltimore, familiar sights—the skyline, the decrepit (but sacred) Stadium Lounge on Greenmount Avenue, the uninhabited Junior Press on Towson's York Road—remind me that everything is just as I left it the last time.

But it's not just as I left it.

The simplest analysis forces me to draw a parallel to my own demise and that of the Orioles. Unrealized potential and completely wasted summers, winters, relationships—they all add up. But I'm going to keep pressing forward, firm belief and unaltered methods my staples. I have no regrets. None. To my mind, these experiences—gone awry or not—have been lessons learned. My primary rebuttal to my self-admonishing is that as long as I do not hurt anybody, the moment is gone.

What if I had less fun in school? Might I be more gainfully employed or, better yet, highly sought by suitors in any town I wished to reside?

It's very possible—in fact, probable.

But at what price? Would self-coddling have prevented the realization of certain experiences?

Also, very probable. And in a world where the clocks cannot be wound backward, I'll choose to do as I did. Again and again. As I make repeated pilgrimages to Baltimore, I am becoming keenly aware that employment opportunities are fleeting. I haven't—and won't—let that deter me.

I have other worries. Most are insignificant with remedies at the ready. Those that continue to lurk, well, I can only keep searching for the answers. Or at least a revelation that they are not at all worth worrying about. This twisted existence has made my every concern a baseball-related one. Oh, analogies can be drawn to dissect and reveal possible problems on a much larger scale.

But baseball is what I understand best.

17

To the casual fan (oh, if life were that simple), the fine print on the reverse of a ticket wears no disguise. In legal terms, you're told of what constitutes a legal game and what you're entitled to should the game be postponed before it becomes official.

Missing, though, are caveats that, should they be heeded, might prevent the faint of heart from ever attending a baseball game.

Where does it convey, for example, that viewing this event may be significantly damaging to your spirit? The proper, uncensored version should accurately read something like this:

> Major League Baseball assumes no responsibility for any emotional stress incurred when viewing this game. Please be advised that the event may be a lengthy one during which expectations of an ultimate triumph may be warranted, but if such prospects do not come to fruition, the bearer of this ticket is subject to (repeated) disappointment in (but not limited to) his/her heroes, managers/coaches, starters, relief pitchers, city, self, and fellow fans. In extreme instances, this game can and will break your fucking heart. Enjoy.

The preceding is the only warning I ever needed. Now I'm not claiming that had I been aware of such pratfalls before I ever attended an Orioles game that I would have steered clear of the whole thing.

But it's nice to be cautioned.

I think of panaceas—all of them my own concoctions, and all of them devised after the fact. Said Søren Kierkegaard: "Life can only be understood backwards; but it must be lived forwards."

And I drift back to my Orioles past, specifically, 1981, when all was right with the Birds and baseball—at least on the surface.

18

Independence and self-sufficiency among my character attributes at sixteen, I began to behave more and more as I would in my adult life. I landed my first job (other than my newspaper routes). A dishwasher at Fox's Beverly Pub on Chicago's South Side, I kept to myself for the most part but did befriend one of the cooks, one Cleveland Bryant. My decision to converse with Mr. Bryant was based on one thing: he looked like Eddie Murray.

He really did. While he lacked the large afro, Cleveland's facial hair matched Murray's almost identically. Resemblance to Murray aside, I had made a wise choice. First and foremost, the content of our conversations was exclusively baseball related, but unlike any locals with which I attempted to talk baseball, this guy had a much broader scope. And he knew Baltimore baseball. Not just Brooks and Frank, but all of it. In fact, he made the claim that while working downtown at the Executive House, he was introduced to and got high with Lee May. I, of course, had no idea if this was true, but I had no reason to doubt it. Aside from myself and this cook who claimed to have smoked some weed with the man, nobody in Chicago knew who Lee May was.

It was 1981. Things were going well for my Birds. In late May, the Yankees went to Baltimore and got slapped around good. From my location, the quickest source was sports phone. While this offered none of the images and live feeds we're inundated with today, it had a certain charm to it—one I kind of miss, in fact. What I learned about the sweep of the Yankees was that in one of the games, Mark Belanger hit a home run—off Ron Guidry. If I remember correctly, it hit the foul pole. Not only was it Belanger's last career home run, but it was also his first in four years. Imagine how I swelled with pride to hear a recorded message detailing an Orioles rout of the Yankees and a home run from the most unlikely source. One cannot help but immediately picture the crowd, the mayhem—Belanger in a home run trot. You can envision it any way you like, and each version puts you in that humid, electric setting on Thirty-third Street.

It's called theater of the mind, and unfortunately, people know less and less about it.

But for every enticing mental image, there is at least one bad one. Fast-forward less than three weeks and we come to June 12. The Orioles lost in Seattle (judging from the box score, it was a less-than-stellar outing) to remain in somewhat of a funk. Worse, still, was the fact that Major League Baseball players were about to stage a strike of unprecedented length. Regarding the reasons for the stoppage of play, I knew then exactly what I know now: player's union, free agency, disagreement with owners. And I am unable to expand on any of these "bullet" points. I only know that this was all I heard while I waited for two agonizing months.

The season resumed (in an unpopular "split-season" format), but all that did was plant one "what-if" after another. Especially where Baltimore was concerned. Scott McGregor was in top form when the interruption hit. He had just pitched a three-hitter against Oakland with Rickey Henderson collecting all of the hits. I'm not sure any team touches a guy with that kind of stuff—not for a month or two, anyway. Additionally, was 1981 Eddie Murray's statement season? It damn sure would have been. As it was, he paced the American League in both home runs and RBI—and still was snubbed in the MVP balloting. With a full season worth of numbers, I doubt that the knights of the keyboard could have denied No. 33, no matter how insolent he may have been.

I'm not hesitant in the least to say I don't understand the details of the 1981 players' strike or the 1994 players' strike. Suffice it to say, there was a tremendous amount of greed involved. It is not my job to comprehend high finance. I'm a Baltimore Orioles fan.

19

My junior year of high school had arrived, and that meant (at my guidance counselor's urging) a search for higher education institutions.

While about two-thirds of confused teens in the halls of St. Laurence weighed the pros and cons of the University of Illinois (for those with decent grades) and of Moraine Valley Community College (for those with decent grades, a pacifier, and a morbid fear of traveling more than four miles from their front doors), mine was merely a choice of what was close in proximity to Memorial Stadium. I looked it over. College of Notre Dame appealed to me. Good location, good academic programs.

Appealing, indeed! It was an all-girls school.

Weighing all the options, Towson State University was a quick and easy choice. The No. 8 bus would take me straight down York Road to Greenmount Avenue and baseball heaven. No further questions. Where do I sign?

Content with my decision (and positive I would be with my future), I found that things went well for me for the remainder of my stay in Chicago. I had, after all, the equivalent of a pardon from the governor. Oh, my peers were satisfied too—for the moment, that is. Only I seemed to know that they—every one of them—would wake up one day and ask aloud, "What have I missed?"

We all had our chances.

The 1982 baseball season revealed a great deal. While it was already etched in concrete that the American League East contained what were by far the strongest specimens, something came—subtly—to the forefront in 1982. And again in 1983. Over the past decade or so, at separate intervals, the division powers were readily identifiable. But one by one, the Yankees, Red Sox, and Brewers had, at times, descended (even if only temporarily) into the subheading of "mediocre."

But not Baltimore.

Two things were evident by 1982: (1) the race for the AL East crown was going to be a bloodbath, and (2) Baltimore was going to be one of the primary combatants. Sure enough, in the waning days of the regular season, there they were stalking the front-running Brewers (who the O's virtually owned in head-to-head play that year). Heads above water for as long as they could possibly manage, the Orioles found themselves three games out of first entering the final weekend.

Friday's twi-night doubleheader sweep provided good indication that my $10 wager with classmate Stan Sterna just might be a profitable one. For my part, all I needed was for Baltimore to sweep a four-game series against the first-place Brewers.

On Saturday, NBC aired Game 3—an 11-3 blowout. In roughly twenty-four hours, the Orioles had gone from three games out, on the brink of elimination, to dead even.

One game to play. Winner takes all.

The Hall of Fame mound matchup of Palmer versus Sutton was most appropriate—and provided a similar sidebar (in my own qualified opinion) matching the showdown between Murray and Yount.

We'll never find out for certain, but my contention is that whoever prevailed that day was going to have (obviously) the division title, but with it the American League's Cy Young Award winner (Palmer or Pete Vuckovich) and the league MVP (Murray or Yount).

Yount struck first, taking Palmer deep. Palmer simply didn't have it that day; but in hindsight, if I had it to do over a thousand times, I'd hand Palmer the ball a thousand times. I loved the matchup then, and I'd love it again and again—class personified against a cheater. Who knows how much (if anything) Sutton got away with that afternoon. But the fact is, he earned the moniker "Black and Decker" for good reason. Additionally, aside from being disappointed by the loss to Sutton, I've always thought he was both opinionated and full of himself in subsequent decades. I recall when Michael Jordan was in one of his hoops sabbaticals and tried his hand at baseball. Jordan had a spot with a Chicago White Sox lower-level team, the Birmingham Barons (I'm pretty sure they were a single-A outfit). Sutton, being the all-knowing and honest guy he is, openly ripped Jordan, arguing that in his experimental phase, he was taking a roster spot from someone who likely deserved it more.

I have news for you, Don: if you're the unfortunate soul who would have filled the *last* roster spot on a single-A team, I doubt you should blame Michael Jordan for blocking your way to Cooperstown.

The finality of that game and the 1982 season was multifaceted. For starters, after trailing, 3-0, the O's answered with a solo home run off the bat of Glenn Gulliver. It was his first and last Major League home run. More importantly, it marked the (temporary) retirement of Earl Weaver. The adjustment for me there was not unlike coming to grips with the reality that there was no Santa Claus. Not that I recall any trauma over learning the truth about St. Nick, but I had always assumed he would get Christmas done every December.

Now I had to depend on someone else.

20

In its final chapter, my high school existence was anything but typical. But it was far from eventful either. Socially, my four years were vacant by my own choosing. Even lunch period—the lone respite from the daily grind of lectures and note-taking—was spent in the library reading that day's newspaper. And it wasn't as though I kept myself completely isolated. I conversed with a few classmates pretty regularly. But for the most part, I didn't like where I was, nor did I enjoy the company of the people I was with. I did anything I could to appear nonconfrontational but get on their collective last nerve at the same time. I began listening to nothing but R & B (and liking it). But the end-all, system-bucking defiance of all conformity was my volunteer efforts in the Harold Washington Chicago mayoral campaign. If there were two things unwelcome on the Southwest Side of Chicago, they were, in order: a black mayor and a fan of any team other than the White Sox.

I had my own agenda for sports and politics. Never would I follow the mindless flock simply because of my zip code or my elders' opinions. I never listened to any mayoral debates or read the local columnists' takes on who stood for what. I was ignorant to the political and social issues, as well (so too, in my opinion, are most voters). My stance was this: Eddie Murray was my favorite baseball player. So why not a black mayor, too?

And high school sweethearts? Sure, I had one: Linda Ellerbee of the NBC nightly news. An intelligent lady with glasses. It didn't hurt that while I watched her, I was only waiting for the network's Major League updates at a time when Baltimore had few peers. She held my interest far more than did any of the Queen of Peace (St. Laurence's neighboring school) girls I rode to and from school with every day on CTA busses. This sort of thing drew my mom's ire. It was clear by now that this Orioleism was no passing phase. It was only getting stronger, in fact. Stronger as in, when they lost, I would often go right to bed in silent fits of anger and frustration—at times, as early as nine on a weekend night.

My lifestyle was promptly compared to those of my brothers and sister. They go out, they have friends, you can't keep doing this, blah-blah-blah.

As for Linda Ellerbee, well, the only plea I got there was to stop watching her—and Johnny Carson and Tom Snyder. In short, my mother had a horrific time trying to wake me for school every morning, and my wee-hours television habit was the culprit.

All told, though, we coexisted nicely. I graduated high school—and bet John Segrue $50 on graduation night that Baltimore was going to win the 1983 World Series (where the fuck is my money, John).

All that remained were three months before I was rightfully transplanted to the Baltimore soil I had sought for some time now. My activities didn't expand much beyond Orioles radio broadcasts and a day-to-day countdown before I took flight.

Oh, I did try out for a traveling baseball team. Then I got cut. Then someone couldn't commit. Then I got "uncut." It was fun, a nice way to cut ties with my younger brother and a couple of good friends. I remember my first at-bat. It was at Morgan Park High School, and I lined a single up the middle. (I also caught a fly ball in left field—a routine fly ball, but who gives a shit, I caught it.) Knowing full well that my talents on the diamond were limited to, well, catching routine fly balls and an occasional lucky single, I made the most of it, mockingly signing autographs all that week at practice and inscribing "1.000" next to my name.

That was, incidentally, my last-ever hit in an organized baseball game. And I don't see another one coming any time soon.

21

When I recall the 1983 season, I'm not quite sure how the hell we won. For starters, Mike Flanagan was off to a lights-out start (I think he was 6-0) when he tore a muscle in May and went on the shelf for a long, long time. And talk about streaky. It seemed that Weaver's teams always avoided the lengthy losing streaks. Joe Altobelli, however, was not immune to such hardships. Not once, but twice, the '83 Orioles endured a seven-game skid. The latter one occurred in August. Literally days away from moving to Baltimore, I attended back-to-back losses at Comiskey Park that extended the streak to six and seven games, respectively.

I don't recall worrying too much. Maybe the '83 team *was* that good. Out to the mound on a Saturday night with the team mired in a losing streak that threatened to reach eight, one Bill Swaggerty got the start—his first ever—and immediately showed that he was bred in a pitching-deep franchise. I don't think Swaggerty got the decision that night, but I know we won, and his name is permanently etched in my mind—within the same portal that holds the names Drungo Hazewood, Mark Corey, Dallas Williams, and Tom Chism. While those guys were "can't miss" prospects, Swaggerty *didn't* miss.

Not on that hot August night when it mattered more than most of us will ever remember.

What transpired the following afternoon constitutes my last recollection of my first life; that is, my childhood and adolescent years in Chicago. While I'm positive there were heartfelt departing hugs, kisses, and well wishes, I honestly don't recall them. And that's not to say that I didn't value my family and their sentiments because I did. I do. My mother made sacrifices for us that I am and will always be incapable of matching. My younger brother has always been not only my best friend but someone to whom I look up. It doesn't matter that I'm two years his senior, his loyalty and values are more refreshing than the traits of any other person I've ever known.

Memories of their gestures tend to vanish over time—as I'm sure that conversely, my own do as well. But a Sunday afternoon game in the heat of a pennant race, now that's gonna linger. Everything about the game set a precedent for Baltimore's survival. Carlton Fisk had a home run turned into a double, which drew the fury of White Sox manager Tony LaRussa. The grand finale, however, was the most satisfying act. With the O's clinging to a 2-1 lead in the bottom of the ninth, the Sox loaded the bases with nobody out—only to have Tim Stoddard strike out two batters and induce a game-ending ground ball from the last hitter.

It was the kind of day that, when it came to an end, I wanted to call perfect.

Perfect, however, was about to come my way in Baltimore. Definitively.

22

With as many belongings as I could possibly check on an hour-and fifty-minute flight, I boarded a Jimmy's taxicab at BWI Airport. Transported to the southwest corner of York Road and Burke Avenue, I climbed the stairs of Scarborough Hall to my third-floor room. My agenda was strict in that friends would come easy in a coed dorm, but my only concern regarding first impressions had to do with the outcome of the Orioles-Twins game at Memorial Stadium that night. I was assured, not having met a single person, that all things social and academic were going to take shape. Nothing was going to stop the Orioles and nothing (other than the 102-degree heat and stifling humidity) was going to interfere with my well-being.

The first person I met was my roommate, Jimmy Connolly. Nice guy from the Washington, D.C. area and friends with Melanie and Teresa who lived downstairs. What I remember about Jimmy—to this day—is that the exchange for his home phone number was 721 (there was a 721 formula in some tire advertisement that made that stick in my mind). Never really got to know much more than that, though. He and his (serious, I guess) girlfriend had some issues with his being away; and after about three or four days, he never came back (to the dorm, anyway). So I had the room to myself.

Acquaintances became friends, bonds (some that have remained to this day) formed, and my personal skills were none for the worse after a guarded existence in my native Chicago.

Simultaneously, the Orioles ran away and hid with the American League East title. No longer in enemy territory, I was free to be as zealous as I wished as September call-up John Stefero delivered walk-off hits in the same unflappable demeanor as Eddie Murray.

Back home, meanwhile, the White Sox secured their own division title by a record twenty games. A showdown was to ensue with sentiments definitively split between myself and anyone I remained in correspondence with in Chicago.

Their own swagger and "winning ugly" bandwagon may have seemed warranted—to them. But I welcomed them, both the team and its fans, as opponents of which I was quite certain we could dispose. Personal bias and loyalty aside, I needed only one telling statistic on which to base my confident opinion: The Chicago White Sox had not played against a team with a .500 or better record since mid-August.

Welcome to Baltimore.

In four games, the White Sox managed just three runs against the Orioles' superior pitching.

Having been a spectator at Games 1 and 2, I spent Sunday night, October 9, in the Memorial Stadium parking lot in anticipation of World Series tickets. I had roughly eleven hours to decide whether to buy tickets for Games 1 and 7 or for Games 2 and 6 at their face value of $25 apiece (the approximate cost of two beers and two hot dogs today).

Unaware of the divine intervention that influenced my decision, I chose Games 2 and 6.

The Birds lost Game 1, 2-1, leaving me to witness to the long ball antics of John Lowenstein and the unhittable offerings of Mike Boddicker on the very next night. Game 6 never happened. It was over in orderly fashion after the Orioles swept the three contests in nearby Philadelphia.

The fare that Sunday night on my college campus—and all over Baltimore—was one of unrestrained celebration and redemption for 1979, 1980, 1981, and 1982. To that very date, I had dutifully complied with the rules and regulations regarding alcohol. With no conscious plans to do anything but adhere to the codes of age and abstinence, I boarded the No. 8 bus for Memorial Stadium. En route from Philadelphia, the Orioles' own bus was scheduled to arrive there at approximately 9:00 p.m. The heroes arrived, the crowd screamed, a parade-like atmosphere (albeit in the dark) was prevalent, and all was good up and down Thirty-third Street.

And then, up pulled a white 1965 Ford Galaxie.

23

Trends in fashion apply to apparel, hairstyles, music, and cars. It matters not what's considered en vogue in other categories. People are going to choose what they like. But as for the aforementioned four avenues, it's completely amazing how the masses will choose a particular style solely to conform with a consensus statement.

Adam Wyatt, the proud owner and operator of the sizable vehicle that slowed after one of the passengers spotted me on Thirty-third Street, was anything but a conformist. To Adam, the Ford Galaxie was a thing of beauty. In retrospect, it was—even as I piled in on that fateful October night. Vaguely familiar with Wyatt and his roommate, Josh Welsh, it was established that, yes, I lived in Scarborough Hall; yes, Adam and Josh knew me from Newell Dining Hall; and yes, I would love to go back to their dorm for an impromptu party.

Rides from strangers were different in 1983. A lot of things were different in 1983.

I was to quickly learn a few basics regarding Josh and Adam. First and fittingly, this *was* an impromptu party—as were the subsequent gatherings five or six nights per week for the next four years. In Newell Hall, at their apartment on Venus Court (a space-themed complex in a not-so-desirable section of Baltimore), in their apartment/room at Mrs. Tear's across the street from the campus, wherever Josh and Adam lived, you'd experience howling laughter, unbelievable yarns, girls, and always, always, *always* beer. Neither one of these guys was an athlete (unless you count getting shit-faced as an

Olympic event). With contrasting personalities, they had one mission: to have fun.

Josh is easy to define as someone who never had a serious moment in his life. Adam, on the other hand, was somewhat of an intellect whose opinions were anything but secret. He hated hippies, and he enjoyed perils of death and mass destruction.

These were my new friends who, fittingly, introduced me to another new friend that night. It's a good bet that his name was Wiedeman, Natty Boh, or Piels. By the end of the night, I didn't know anyone's name, including my own. Sickened by the very mention of beer for about two weeks that followed my inaugural intake, I didn't exactly "vow" to swear off the golden liquid, but I did conclude that it was something I was glad I finally tried but would not be able to stomach on any regular basis. I have what I consider an innate gift (one of very few): I have the capability to view something, in liquid or solid form, and immediately determine if it's any good. Hence, I have long since eliminated spinach, peas (anything green), mustard, onions, tomatoes, bananas (to name a few) from my diet. Now I have unwillingly sampled some of these only to confirm my suspicions of how awful they taste, but for the most part, I'm already assured of their crappiness—without tasting.

I was wrong about beer, though. More than a quarter century later, I absolutely adore beer.

Such was the reward that I made a conscious decision to seize—but only after realizing world championship status on the diamond.

24

So this is what it was all about, at long last—World Series champions.

As we're inundated with doctrine, gospel, fables, prescriptions, lessons, advice, and suggestions from the time we can take a piss on our own, each of us, many times, is fed what we instantly deem a crock of shit as we're told, "Winning isn't everything."

I sit here today, looking back on my every last baseball experience, and I can honestly profess that winning is *not* everything.

Don't misconstrue this message. I shall not forget watching as Cal Ripken, Jr. snared a soft line drive for the final out on October 16, 1983, and the entire Orioles team spilled out onto the field in celebration. It took a few moments to sink in, but I was truly ecstatic, looking for someone, something—anything—to hug. And that was pretty much it. Of course, bragging rights are the standard accessory to a World Series title. You'll talk about it all winter, all next season, and in the matter of the 1983 Baltimore Orioles, for nearly the next three decades. The fervor, of course, doesn't come close to what you experienced on championship night. Anyone who tells you that his or her team won the series and they were on a high for any more than the remainder of that night is a liar.

In the matter of winning a World Series, like the vast majority of time-consuming conquests, the chase is better than the catch.

That being said, I sincerely treasure the memory of that crowning achievement in 1983. I really do. But there are specific moments that I look back on with more genuine fondness, pride, and vivid recollection.

And they all involve losing.

One could argue that this is a comment on the human psyche, citing the "forbidden fruit" principal. But I disagree.

Case by case, I'll put the 1979 World Series, the final weekend of the 1982 season and (while it's perhaps somewhat of a stretch) the final weekend of the 1989 season up against our 1983 Fall Classic triumph.

As for the former event, my biased opinion has the '79 Birds at the top of the list, without rival, of the greatest baseball teams I've ever seen. Now had they taken that last step (they had three chances) and defeated the Pirates, would it have been sweeter than the 1983 victory? I'll never know.

The heart-stopping conclusion to the 1982 season is, by far, my finest moment as an Orioles fan. Three games out of first with four to play and a winner-take-all showdown—like an 1800s Old West gunfight (an occurrence that I am convinced, by the way, actually went down in black-and-white). With the division title, the MVP award and the Cy Young laurel all on the line, the Orioles succumbed, 10-2. Any loss that day would have been devastating (until hurt gave way to pride, which it inevitably did), but this was closer than the final score might indicate. Within 5-2 in the bottom of the eighth, the Orioles had two on, two out, and Joe Nolan at the plate. He hit an opposite-field tailing fly ball to deep left field ("deep" to the 309-foot dimensions, anyway). Brewers outfielder Ben Oglivie made a sprawling grab on the gravel warning track, and you knew it was pretty much our last chance—much like Eddie Murray's bases-loaded fly out to the warning track in the eighth inning of Game 7 in 1979. In both the '79 and '82 decisive games, a squelched Oriole rally was immediately followed by opponents' tack-on runs that left no doubt as to the Orioles' fate.

So the next one will be different. It will.

Analyzing the climates of then and now, it was a given that back in the 1970s and early '80s, the Orioles were pretty much *supposed* to be in the hunt every year. More recently, not so much. Should the Orioles win a title in 2009, I needn't tell you of the potentially riotous ceremonies in Baltimore. And they, too, would eventually cease.

And the next task would be to defend that title or to just do it again. Someday.

25

I remember Mike Gottlieb during my early days at Towson State University. He was Billy Hunter's assistant coach on the Tigers baseball staff. Heavy New York accent, always talked Yankees. So yeah, I'm pretty sure he was a Bronx native. I got to know Mike after landing the position of team statistician/scorekeeper (what else?) in the spring 1984 semester. We disagreed on quite a bit to the point where I'd introduce arguments that were downright ludicrous. Mike Gottlieb knew baseball—much more than I did.

This made it all the more entertaining for me to make ridiculous comparisons (almost always after I made sure I had an audience). One day it began, there we were, comparing franchise greats, position by position. Mike was floored when I put Rick Dempsey up against Thurman Munson.

But he refused to go any further when I put Al Bumbry above DiMaggio.

He was easy to agitate. I recall one time as he pitched batting practice (a duty I believe he actually performed for the Yankees, in fact), he positioned himself behind the protective netting and began to fire away. Well, it wasn't two or three offerings before a would-be delivery ricocheted off the metal framework. The netting device was positioned to protect a right-handed pitcher, and Gottlieb was a southpaw. (Or maybe it was vice versa but, in any event, that's what happened, and he was the butt of jokes for a week.)

But man, did he know baseball.

Shortly after the 1984 season opened, I began to revert to a meaningless regular-season Orioles game from the prior September. It was meaningless because the Orioles had long since clinched the division crown. In somewhat-lax fine-tuning for the postseason, the Orioles fell victim to a three-game sweep at the hands of the Detroit Tigers. Right away, Gottlieb warned of Detroit and its very real potential to unseat the Orioles in 1984.

Making a genius out of Gottlieb, the Tigers won thirty-five of their first forty games in 1984, and the season was pretty much over before it started.

One last side note, though. I ran into Gottlieb near the end of the '84 season with the Orioles about fifteen games out with maybe twenty left to play. I bet him $10 that Baltimore was going to win out and overtake Detroit. Masked by a serious facade, I convinced him that I really believed I had a chance. So he asked me to increase the wager to $20. I quickly replied that I "only wanted to take ten from him" and that the only reason I was making the bet was to show him that "I got balls."

When I again refused to raise the stakes, he replied, "Apparently, you're only going with one nut."

That has to be one of the best lines I ever heard. Especially in that New York accent.

And so blossomed a new side of me. Unaware of the gradual burst from the cocoon that had tight wraps on any verbal communication to which I may have been inclined, I slowly began to announce out loud what I was thinking. I found that in addition to listeners being receptive, some of these "declarations" had an unintentional (at first) comic effect. It did get out of control at times with my fair share of rude comments mixed in. But friendships were realized through these chance conversations that I previously wouldn't have dreamed of initiating.

I fondly remember Zaynep.

Zaynep sat in the Newell Dining Hall, by herself, every night. I'd load my tray, always color coordinating orange soda, milk, and Coca-Cola in transparent plastic cups, showing the proper hues of the Orioles. As I walked toward the back room every night, I'd notice this girl by herself. One night, I just set my tray at her table and sat across from her as if I'd known her my entire life. No awkward introduction or "Hi, is it okay if I join you?"

I just sat and began eating.

She was amused. We began talking, and subsequently, we dined together almost every night. It was never planned. In fact, I don't think I ever saw Zaynep outside the dining hall. When I came to eat, if she was there (which she usually was), we sat together. She was from Turkey and, of course, had an accent. I remember that every night, I'd get a dish of mashed potatoes (still far and away my favorite food selection on any menu). One night as I set my tray down, Zaynep smiled and said, "Look at you, always mashed poratoes."

Mashed "poratoes." To this day, that's what I call them.

26

Less than two calendar years removed from a World Series championship, times were changing in Baltimore. The very structure and elements of the most fundamentally sound franchise in all of American sports were showing signs of mortality. Tapping outside sources, the club signed Fred Lynn between the 1984 and 1985 seasons. This was a productive move. Hell, in one three-day span against Minnesota, the guy hit a home run in the ninth inning of each game. Two months later, he hit a walk-off shot against Chicago in what I consider one of the top three most dramatic comebacks in my experiences as a fan.

But where were the arms? What was left of the 1983 staff was collectively aging. But unlike in decades past, there were no can't-miss prospects in Rochester. You can have power and speed up and down the lineup, but without pitching, there's no chance.

The 1985 team did, in fact, post a winning record. But simply eclipsing the .500 plateau was not enough. While it has become a surprisingly lofty goal in recent seasons, I wasn't ready to accept it as an objective then. Nor will I ever deem .500 an acceptable performance. These are Major League Baseball players—the best in the world. Don't tell me about "rebuilding" or "biding time" or "grooming" players for tomorrow. Go out there and find a way to win now. It can be done.

Such were my sentiments as I awaited the 1986 season.

If you go by the book, which far too many who pose as "historians" do, you'll be quick to cite 1986 as the demise of the Orioles franchise. It represented, after all, the team's first last-place showing in thirty-three otherwise-glorious seasons.

But I challenge each and every skeptic that contrarily, 1986 was a good season. I summon the memory of an early-August *Monday Night Baseball* broadcast. As I wathced from home in Chicago (on summer vacation from Towson), ABC interrupted whoever happened to be playing to show an Orioles highlight. It was an Eddie Murray double that tied a game against the Angels, 2-2. Having shown the Orioles feed, the network then showed a frozen image of Murray as an instrumental portion of a Whitney Houston hit accompanied. When I think of 1986, I don't think of last place, but I think of a team that, on that August night, was within two and a half games of the front-running Red Sox. No other AL East challenger was to get any closer.

A few nights later, with Texas in town, the Orioles hit not one but *two* grand slams in the same game (Jim Dwyer and Jim Traber) and still managed to lose. That touched off a losing skein that never really stopped. The September record was atrocious, and resultantly, we finished dead last for the first time.

But that doesn't negate four-plus months of contending baseball. Not in my book.

*I was there when you were a queen,
And I'll be the last one there beside you.*

—J. D. Souther

27

I'm in my forties now.

This, another on a long ledger of visits to Baltimore, neither confirms nor refutes that the same things that were important to me when I was thirteen are those that define me today.

Other than reactions to the fortunes of your team, there's not much variance that goes with being a baseball fan. All winter long, you look forward to Opening Day. After that inaugural game (provided your team triumphs), you truly believe that your team has the elements it's going to take to win. Win it all. Disappointments ensue (most of the time), and other than relishing the role of spoiler, you address what needs to be done to right the ship the following season—almost always on deaf ears.

Mirroring those trends are my own habits, my repeated sojourns to Baltimore, the frequenting of saloons, and internally rehashing the details—good, bad, and ugly—of recent seasons and distant campaigns, alike. Inherent to this analysis are comparisons. Fueling the process, always, is one beer after another.

Upon literally translating the activities of such nights, the average observer is certain to view the entire series as a repetitive and self-defeating endeavor.

But eternal hope, whether it's warranted or not, is the absolute beauty of baseball. No matter how many consecutive losing seasons Baltimore withstands, there will be solace in the belief that "well, this isn't going to be as bad as the '87 team or the '88 team." While I'll defend the last-place 1986 squad as one that had a good season, I cannot take the same stance regarding the 1987 and 1988 installments.

Have you ever noticed how selective memory influences your views to paint a picture that never represents the whole? Take 1987. I recall the pain of the prior season (at least its final month and a half) and the dire need to get off to a good start. That didn't happen. The Orioles had a bad April and simply weren't good enough to play catch-up. Those April games that set an unfavorable tone were played on some unseasonably cold days and nights at Memorial Stadium.

And that's what I remember about 1987. It's established in the recesses of my mind that the entire 1987 season was played in gloomy weather.

I don't remember one sunny day that year. Maybe there weren't any.

So as for the continued folly of believing that things can and will be better, there you have it. There can't possibly be another year in which the sun never shines.

Delear prius.

28

Undue attention—and the assumption that everything is to be interpreted at face value—plague this world and will continue to do so.

This hypocrisy begins, for me, at the very foundation of Christianity, duplicates itself in every arena, and is readily apparent in baseball "fans."

One need only open a history book or, better yet, turn on any network news broadcast to learn of savage killings, greed, and age-old controversy caused in the name of one or more religious sectors. There are countless faiths. What makes one more correct than another?

I'll explain my theory based on the beliefs instilled in me in a Roman Catholic upbringing. I believe in Jesus Christ. I believe that He was the Son of God. And I believe He was crucified and exited His own tomb three days later. I realize that with each scientific discovery and "advancement," there is definitive explanation for yet another previously unexplained phenomenon. The smarter we get, the less guidance we think we need. When our moment comes—every one of us—we'll instinctively seek God with a horrible fear that just wasn't there back when we thought we knew it all.

When you're on that flight and excessive turbulence rocks the plane back and forth, when you look at that funnel cloud approaching, nearer and nearer, not a single one of you will think about "evolution." No, you'll immediately think of and beg God, wherever He is, to spare you just this one last time.

You're not so smart after all, are you.

I also believe that the Holy Bible and countless structures in which we worship and profess our faith came to be as a direct result of Christ's resurrection. Witnesses to miracles during Christ's time on earth, His followers were not convinced until He performed the ultimate "now you see me, now you don't" trick. And then, it was too late.

So regimented worship, which should've been practiced from Christ's arrival on earth, has been done in hindsight—every bit of it. Scriptures, too, I'm convinced, were penned well after the fact when there was no prophecy involved, only recounting of the facts. And all of religion has since expanded in purpose to one of sucking billions of dollars from victims who believe they can "buy" God's approval. Holding fast to tradition and to the assumption that the current hierarchy is one that was put into place by Christ's own teachings, Catholics are to view the pope as God on earth. I, for one, will not accept a mere mortal as even a vague facsimile of God but, rather, a token whose position was created when people had realized that they had failed their real savior. Failed Him and killed Him. Where was the reverence while Christ walked among us? Was His word not sufficient?

Kindly bear with this rant if you will. I am not a Bible-thumper. I'm far from it. I only wish to ensure that my beliefs aren't halfhearted or subject to misinterpretation. I maintain my faith in a Supreme Presence and in certain earthly institutions. Never, though, will I confuse the two. Hence, I have difficulty with traditions that those around me seem to so readily accept. How many people go to confession? Is a man in a robe (obscured by a wall in a booth) going to absolve me for my sins? Maybe. Maybe the very act prompts forgiveness from God. But I don't think so.

Attending mass, receiving holy communion, offering a sign of "peace" to neighboring parishioners (only when instructed, of course)—these are all simply motions that people routinely practice. I cannot count the number of times I've walked into a church, searched for a pew in which to sit—only to have an elderly woman give me a glance of utter disgust as I asked permission to get past her.

As though she was entitled to the entire pew.

I find fault with Catholicism in that worship is a most regimented procedure. Stand, sit, kneel, one prayer, two prayer, gospel, homily, communion, see you next week, go home, and talk about everybody. Can anybody tell you the essence of what was preached? What was the message? And as for personal prayer, does anyone attempt to communicate with God in anything but dire circumstances? Blind faith is almost nonexistent. Church is not a place of worship—its intended purpose—but a convenience.

Are there any true believers? Or does everyone act in compliance only?

And so it goes with the deserted "temples" that are suddenly filled to capacity when their tenants are in first place. It's as if our duty as fans entails supporting our troops on Opening Day and then a few times later in the season, provided they are within striking distance of first place. In short, while any team's mission statement could be heeded as a promise that efforts are plentiful and lean times will eventually give way to prosperous seasons, unless that team is producing *now*, believers are scarce.

This is how Americans are conditioned: follow the pack and don't ask questions. We ignore the fact that every last nickel of state lottery proceeds is going into somebody's pocket and not toward education and public schools, as promised. We stop at each tollbooth and hand over ever-increasing allotted monetary amounts for the "temporary" institution that was put into effect decades ago to raise money to repair those roads. Have we any idea the exorbitant amount of cash that's forwarded to the tollway authorities every single day? And where it goes?

There are so many do-gooders. There really are. The countless people who brave the elements and city traffic with receptacles in hand, they honestly believe in their collective heart of hearts that the money they collect in exchange for, say, a Tootsie Roll, goes toward finding a cure for muscular dystrophy—or for whichever ailment they're collecting.

Not a dime goes where it's supposed to. I don't think it does. It's my firm contention that those bills and coins, deposited and received (by the initial taker) in good faith, go to the same place as the money we mail to that starving child in Kenya, the same destination as the pledges we assume are going to Jerry's Kids, the same place to which the cash we drop in those firemen's boots goes.

Into somebody's pocket.

That's where I'm going to tell you it goes. And entertaining the possibility that I'm wrong, I'll admit I have no concrete proof of any of this. But my gut tells me that I'm spot-on.

29

Regardless of the state of Major League Baseball throughout its storied timeline, winning wrests public attention more consistently than does anything else. Headline space has been reserved for the likes of Ruth, Mantle, and Reggie. Attention and adoration by the masses is warranted when a team puts a winner on the field.

In 1988, unfortunately, the converse held true.

As if to welcome me into the adult world and punctuate my exile back to my native Chicago, the Orioles set a new mark for futility in the spring of 1988.

Now I cannot claim that I knew Baltimore was going to lose its first twenty-one games that year. No way, never saw it coming. But I can say that it all made sense as unpleasant circumstances and one humiliating defeat after another comprised the daily menu.

It began with a trip to Memorial Stadium for the season opener against Milwaukee. My sister worked for America West Airlines at the time and had given me a buddy pass.

That's where it all started.

Upon my arrival to the airport, I learned that those flying on a buddy pass were required to wear business attire. Didn't have any (still don't). So more than $300 later, I boarded a flight headed for Phoenix, Arizona.

You see, Phoenix was America West's hub, thus all flights—regardless of destination—had to go via Phoenix.

I finally got to Baltimore and met (as planned) with two couples from Towson—both of which happened to be engaged in heated, daylong arguments. The afternoon was tension-filled, and the game was anything *but* tense. Milwaukee pummeled the Orioles, 12-0.

There were very few close games in the Orioles' historic run. And as the streak reached double digits, they were suddenly a skewed version of baseball's darlings. How long would this go on? Each loss set them deeper into the cellar, deeper into embarrassment, and further from the proud tradition that had defined the franchise for about three decades.

As late April unfolded, the O's were in Minnesota and the cover of that week's *Sports Illustrated* read: "0-18: The Agony of the Orioles." On the weekend that approached, Baltimore was headed for Chicago to play a three-game series at Comiskey Park. I can still recall vividly the repetitive questions of everyone who knew of our plight: "Aren't you hoping that they get swept in Minnesota so they'll have a chance to break the streak here?"

No. I'm *not* hoping they get swept, or lose any of the three games in Minnesota. Is that what you'd wish for your own team? Your stupid question bothers me. If you were a baseball fan yourself, you'd never ask such a thoughtless question. If you take even the slightest bit of pride in your team, you'd want it to win on any given day against any given opponent, not to be some fucking sideshow just so you can go watch that first win in person.

The Orioles did, incidentally, get swept in the Twin Cities, setting up a Friday, April 29 contest between themselves—at 0-21—and the Chicago White Sox. In attendance that night, I sat in the upper deck box seats behind home plate, which provided what was far and away the best vantage point at that venue. My father, a Chicago police officer, worked in Sox Security and saw to it that I had those rock-star seats every time I went down there (which was every time Baltimore came calling).

The atmosphere that night was one I had never experienced before, not at Comiskey Park. In glaring contrast to any other game I saw there, this one was attended by an unbiased crowd. Just five seasons earlier, at this very site, the Orioles slammed the door shut on what was to be Chicago's best (and only) chance at a World Series berth since 1959. But memories failed the South Siders that night. The competition took on a new meaning. This was no longer Baltimore, feared American League rival. It was Baltimore, a laughing stock who, almost four weeks into the season, had yet to win a single game. I, for one, was ready for a battle. I didn't want sympathy, I wanted these "fans" to still be pissed about Tito Landrum and 1983. Had the tables been turned, I assure you that I would not have thought it might be "cute" to see the White Sox finally get a win—at our expense, no less.

Apparently, the Oriole players shared my sentiments that night. In a 1979-esque performance, Baltimore beat the White Sox, 9-0. Appropriately, Eddie Murray and Cal Ripken, Jr. each homered, leading the hitting barrage as they had for years prior, in an age of Oriole dominance.

There is nothing cute about losing. Only satisfaction in winning.

30

Nothing, nothing at all improved during the rest of the 1988 season.

A major off-season shake-up began with the trade of Murray. Much like Ripken had been left to question the organization when his father was fired six games into the infamous '88 skid, I sat, dumbfounded, when I learned of Murray's fate. This was my favorite player without rival. Oh, I loved them all, each and every one of them. But this was the cornerstone of the franchise, the man who so ably bridged the gap between the glory of the early '70s and the juggernaut rosters of the late '70s to early '80s.

But there was no finger-pointing, no questioning, no jumping ship. I had to be of the mind-set that Randy Milligan was my new first baseman. Team fortunes first. It wasn't as though our Broadway schedule had been abruptly cancelled. Just a change in cast members. The show must go on.

As the 1989 Grapefruit League season neared a close and I prepared for what was to be my final season opener at Memorial Stadium, word of Roger Clemens' predictions spread. Fast. Clemens, the Boston Red Sox scheduled starter for the season opener in Baltimore, candidly told the media that he was going to not only beat the Orioles, but also no-hit them in the process. While that's a bold and ill-advised statement for anyone to make, it turned out to be just the first in a series of actions that Clemens took that have made me hate his guts far beyond what I could ever convey on a printed page. He did not, incidentally, no-hit the Orioles that afternoon. In fact, as soon as Maryland-bred Joan Jett finished her rendition of the National Anthem, the Birds took to hitting Clemens pretty hard. A three-run homer off the bat of Ripken closed the books on Clemens' outing—which didn't resemble a no-hitter in the least. And after Boston answered with a single run to tie the game at 4-4, the Orioles held the BoSox at bay and proceeded to win in extra innings.

The headline in the sports section of the next day's *Baltimore Sun* read, "0-21? Not This Year."

And so began an adventure, a series of baby steps, the completion of each instilling another morsel of faith in a roster that, on paper, didn't stand a snowball's chance in hell.

It was early, but first place was ours, and immediately the consensus thought was that these overachievers on Thirty-third Street would soon come crashing back to earth and give way to those fitting the description of contenders.

And they waited.

Someone forgot to inform the five-hundred-to-one Orioles that they didn't belong. As the summer months unfolded, it was clear that first place was not a rest stop or a four-hour nap at a motel. It was a residence in which this team was quite comfortable.

Pushing forward, it became a race that prompted condition-based questions: how many days are left in the season, and how many more games are we going to have to win? If there was the slightest lack of swagger in Baltimore's statement that year, it stemmed from the fact that, save for Ripken, none of these guys knew what a pennant race was.

A telltale sign of inexperience, the Orioles earned a dubious and unusual distinction that summer by enduring the longest-ever losing streak (eight games) by a first-place team that remained in first place at the streak's conclusion. But by early September, our stranglehold on first place—a grip that had progressively loosened—was gone. Momentum had swiftly gone north of the border, specifically, to the Toronto Blue Jays.

As the pages fell from the calendar, all that remained for Baltimore were dim hopes—and the ingenious scheduling that had the Orioles spending the final weekend of the season at the SkyDome. Stay close and see what happens.

Entering the Friday night contest trailing by one game, the Orioles opened the festivities in the worst possible manner: Phil Bradley led off the game with a home run.

At the risk of sounding facetious, I'll tell the world that I didn't like Bradley's home run that night (well, the timing of it, anyway) and that I despise all first-batter home runs as they are launched. I've seen them numerous times, and it almost always represents the last run your team is going to score all night.

Such was the case in Canada that night. Orioles closer and 1989 Rookie of the Year Greg Olson allowed the Blue Jays to tie it on a eighth-inning wild pitch, and with no access from my Chicago apartment, I could only watch the Cubs-Cardinals game and hope for a pleasing update. Instead, I got word from the slurred voice of Harry Caray that Toronto won in extra innings. And suddenly, two games remained, and they were both must-wins.

Combatants the following afternoon in the last-ever NBC Game of the Week, the Orioles appeared primed to bring the matter to the final day. Getting the start was Baltimore native Dave Johnson, a right-hander who, approaching his thirtieth birthday, had all of four Major League wins to his credit.

On this day, however, this common-named man fit the mold of Oriole pitchers past, yielding just two hits through seven innings. Having departed with a 3-1 lead, Johnson watched, expressionless, from his vantage point in the Oriole dugout as Toronto hitters reached two Oriole relievers for three of the quickest runs you'll ever see.

It was over.

Somewhere along the way, billboards in Baltimore read "Why Not?" and the citizens readily embraced a youthful crop that gave everyone but Toronto, more than they could handle. It wasn't a pitching-rich squad like the ones that were an Orioles trademark throughout the 1960s and 1970s. But in its own way, the 1989 version smacked of Baltimore.

31

Spoiled by talent-laden rosters in seasons past, I had guarded expectations following the 1989 season. As always, they were high expectations but somewhat hollowed, nonetheless. It's one thing to aim for October after you've been nipped at the wire the previous season. But an overachieving season is, by common definition, a onetime thing. If you look through the pages of your baseball bibles, you'll find that more often than not, a team that just comes out of nowhere to contend does so because of career years by multiple players, down seasons for expected contenders, and above all else, luck.

The encore usually isn't something to write home about.

As 1990 approached, I was about as out of place as the Orioles were the summer before. Contrarily, though, I was underachieving and not at all concerned about it. I landed a job with a firm called Jacobson Publishing. In a small office in downtown Chicago, I cut and pasted (literally, in a pre-computer era) sales reports for heavy native steer, Holsteins, and a few other livestock names that escape my memory, never to return.

It wasn't working very well, my trainer saw immediately that I didn't give a shit, and my days were numbered from the start. I knew this. Then one day, a friend phoned from Baltimore and told me that an English-born friend of hers was headed from Baltimore to Seattle via Amtrack and was making a three-hour stop in Chicago. Could I meet and entertain this young lady? Sure, I agreed.

Just blocks from my office, I met her at the train station and asked what she felt like doing.

"I could do with a drink," was her reply in a heavy British accent.

Adhering to her wish, I did with a drink myself and, three hours later, headed home, having never reported back to the office. The next morning, a severance check and a good-bye awaited me. I wasn't proud of what I had done (or had failed to do). But I wasn't concerned over it, either.

The Orioles' performance that summer reflected my own. It began with that auspicious start in Kansas City. In an eleven-inning duel on Opening Day, Sam Horn went four for five with two three-run homers, and the O's prevailed, 7-6. If ever there was a halo effect, there was one for Sam Horn that year. Literally hours into the season, he was a mortal lock for the Triple Crown. Things slowed, of course (dramatically), but just based on that one performance, he was expected to do something remarkable every time he suited up. That was my anticipation, anyway.

And throughout the season, the wasted potential sapped my emotions. We'd get near .500, lose a few, get back to .500, lose a few more. But all the while, Baltimore stayed within striking distance, within four games as late as August. Nothing ever came of it, though. No serious statement in the form of a winning streak or dramatic comeback. The whole thing was as inspiring as my unemployment checks that summer. Sure, I was alive and getting paid; but as the rest of the world was out accomplishing something, anything, I sat idle. This wasn't a spell of any length to speak of, but unsettling, nonetheless. Not having a purpose (albeit briefly) was killing me, twisting my soul as though it was a wet towel.

A quick chain of events later, I got busy.

32

With new experiences come new lifestyles.

In early 1991, still unemployed at this juncture, I stepped outside to go meet a friend at a bar near Chicago's Wrigley Field. I wasn't forty yards from my apartment building when I felt and heard quick footsteps approaching me. I quickly turned and saw two young guys who, judging from their expressions and rapid invasion of my space, were after me.

One of them pulled on my leather jacket. As I grabbed the panel from his grip and began to spin away, the other one pointed a gun about three inches from and in the direction of my face.

This was an obstacle. Still fresh in my memory are the basic facts pertaining to that little stickup. I venture to say that I wasn't prepared for it—or for anything like it. I've never been a fan of confrontation, let alone a showdown of this magnitude. Item by item, they took, at gunpoint: my jacket, a gold chain (though the attached charm, which I still have, descended down the front of my shirt when he violently yanked the chain off my neck), and finally, the cash that was in my front pocket. It wasn't much more than $20, but there was an old two-dollar bill included. Perhaps what spared my life that night was my Walkman. The headphones were resting on my neck when one of the thieves grabbed the cassette player. In the transfer, the thing fell to the ground, and the tape came out. The commotion and resultant noises sparked some sort of panic because one of them immediately sprinted away and his partner, of course, followed. In retrospect, for that little bit of ruckus to scare them off, I don't think they were going to kill me.

Now, had they remained calm and glanced at the *Gershwin Plays Gershwin* tape I had been listening to, I do, in fact, believe I would've been shot and slain on the spot. This was a wake-up call of sorts. I wasn't overwhelmed with fright. No, actually, a few years later I hit a deer on Super Bowl Sunday, and *that*, I will admit, scared the shit out of me. As for my victim role in the cold nighttime neighborhood holdup, I was maybe pissed off a little bit, but nothing in the realm of terrified.

Baseball was just a few weeks away, and it was time to get a job. It was time to retrieve that fervor I had known as I planned to experience all things Baltimore. I had to put into motion a concerted effort to find employment—something rewarding, something with meaning.

And I had to get out of that neighborhood which, in itself, wasn't particularly bad but was too crowded, had easy access to major byways, and most of all, was way too convenient for dregs like the ones who assaulted me to come from wherever they did, with criminal activity their sole intent, and get in and out unnoticed.

My eternal source of hope listened to pleas—most of them justified—of a perfect world in which I would be employed at a racetrack. I knew the sport (the sport of kings is horse racing's lofty moniker), I knew the vernacular, I knew of the vagabond types that frequented the ovals, and I knew the money was good.

Supportive, as always, my mother called a contact in the harness-racing circles, and the job was mine. Offtrack betting parlors were about to sprout up all over the Chicago area, and I was in the first crop of pari-mutuel tellers at the newly opened 111th Street facility.

I was good at it, taking wagers at a lightning-fast pace and was often tipped accordingly. Somewhat like Baltimore, this place became a friendly haven with friendly strangers. As in Baltimore, I befriended people of whom my family and friends had no knowledge. Every day, I got into my car and drove to my separate existence. And from all of *these* people, I found yet another hideaway in my new place of residence and its inviting surrounding elements.

Specifically, I found an apartment near Midway Airport. About two blocks due west, a saloon beckoned almost nightly. No name, no marquee, no neon beer signs. Just a private club. I had heard about the place from a couple generations of my own family. As close to storybook as you could possibly come, this place had both of the features of vital importance to a bar: in order, gambling and beer. It was anything but typical in that I don't think I ever heard any of the patrons ever mention the word "bookie." This was with good reason. "Bookie" implies a telephone contact. This place was no such operation. The communication here was face-to-face, exactly as if you were in a casino sports book. You read the odds, told the man who you liked (and how much you liked them), and physically put your cash on the bar.

Between this bar and the OTB, the inherent dangers were plenty, but not for me. While I'm to this day void of a lot of the skills and traits that I wish I possessed, here, I was able to practice the most important of all virtues: discipline. At the racetrack, the policy was that the tellers were not supposed to make wagers. The only time this was enforced, however, was when a teller made and lost more bets than he/she could pay for (this happened all the time). And even then, the slap-on-the-wrist "punishment" rendered was that the teller could come back to work as soon as he/she made good with the racetrack money room.

My advantage in the horse racing industry was that I had seen far too much of what it can do and was able to heed the self-warning. Horse betting is not betting on a baseball game or a football game. There are ten or eleven races on a card, and with simulcasting (which came our way shortly after the place opened), there are literally hundreds of live races every day. Add to the tall odds of steady success that there are at least eight horses (on the average) in every race. The likelihood of consistency (positive consistency, that is) is minute. And it leads to chasing money, race after race after race.

I've heard it professed that subconsciously, many gamblers *want* to lose. The theory goes something to the effect of "feed someone enough shit, and they acquire a taste for it."

With so many people I've encountered—and not just at the racetrack—this diagnosis rings true.

Embraced by my racetrack bosses who saw delight with the direct link between my services and an increased handle, I was given a token "scolding" (they sent me home one day) for going to my car between races to check on baseball scores. Much more serious discipline, however, was warranted for a separate stunt.

On one particularly slow Sunday night, I sat and conversed with another teller (my union steward, actually) about fluctuation of the racetrack odds. I was told that a sizable wager at one of the lesser tracks (oh, say, Balmoral Park harness racing) would turn the odds completely upside down.

I made that sizable wager, saw the odds alter dramatically, then cancelled the ticket, and watched as the odds "unchanged"—again, dramatically.

I did this no fewer than three times.

I honestly didn't know the magnitude of my "transactions." I certainly had no intent to "deceive the public." But with members from the Illinois Racing Board and suits from Balmoral Park immediately on the phone in panic, that's the lecture I was subject to for the ensuing days. I was forced to immediately close my window. The next day, three Racing Board executives paid a personal visit and walked me around the facility in search of this "big bettor" whom I had described as "a white guy (of which there were virtually none at 111th Street) who looked kinda like Santa Claus."

From that experience, I learned that seeking Orioles updates while on the clock is a far less serious offense than (in the stern warning of the authorities) "catering to someone who wants to fuck with the odds."

That incident aside, gambling was, like any other institution or vice I can bring to mind, something with which I didn't get involved—unless it involved Baltimore.

And so it came to be, in the West Lawn neighborhood on Chicago's South Side, that a racetrack employee with an otherwise-habit-free life began to bet on the Baltimore Orioles. Every night. And while the 1991 Orioles fared only slightly better than some of the worst versions in club history, I wasn't exactly in financial straits as a result. Not at $25 per game. This is the beauty of casino-style sports wagering: when forced to front the money, you'll find you have less and less balls (at least I did, anyway). Betting over the telephone is a different thing, a dangerous thing. I don't recommend the latter to anyone, regardless of their financial status.

In the later portion of 1991, I was equal parts hopeful and sad. Check that, a better way to describe the latter emotion might be "resigned to the notion that I am powerless against inevitable change." The hope came in the form of a memorable performance I witnessed one Sunday afternoon at Comiskey Park. There, I watched a young Stanford University product named Mike Mussina make his Major League debut. I'm definitely no scout, nor would I ever pretend to be one. And from my vantage point well down the first-base line, I could not begin to experience the velocity and variety of Mussina's pitches that day. But I got a gut inclination from the first inning that this kid was something special. All told, he yielded a solo home run to Frank Thomas and maybe a single to Joey Cora. And that was all it took to spoil his effort because White Sox veteran Charlie Hough blanked the Orioles altogether. Down, 1-0 late, Red Sox castoff Dwight Evans came up with the bases loaded and hit a scorching line drive only to have Hough stick his glove out and snare it.

Despite the setback, the afternoon set itself apart as a silver lining to an otherwise-dismal season—and the bleak prospect of life without Memorial Stadium.

I've missed weddings to which I've been invited and had RSVP'd affirmatively. I've missed wakes and funerals of relatives—my paternal grandfather included (though, in my defense, I got lost on an unfamiliar route to that event). For these "oversights," if you will, I make no excuses. Each time, it was a shitty and disrespectful thing to do. But as the 1991 season wound down, my priorities would allow no such absence in the matter of Memorial Stadium. All I was able to get a ticket for was the Friday night game—the last night game in the Orioles' storied history at the Waverly palace.

I drove from Chicago to Baltimore that day, attended the game, and witnessed an extra-inning loss. That was it. An unceremonious ending to a relationship that got a late start (at least in terms of face-to-face encounters) and came to an abrupt end in favor of something that could not possibly be better.

When a loved one dies, sooner than later, friends and relatives gather (usually before the corpse is even buried) and reminisce about his/her traits, habits, and mannerisms—as if they were all patented. This is undoubtedly the only manner in which Memorial Stadium can be recalled. Sure, there are the repeated tales of the first NFL cheerleaders and marching band, the Weaver versus Santarone tomato contests, and dozens of other tales that are common lore. But I'll cherish its memory for countless other reasons. The stifling humidity, the view of the shrubbery beyond the outfield fences (from the other side of the tall chain-link fence) as you prepared to enter the stadium or, as I often did, simply circled the edifice for your own viewing enjoyment. These were among the things I loved about the structure itself.

And there were additional aesthetically pleasing elements in the surrounding area. I loved the Olympic Lounge on Greenmount. I enjoyed the walks from the bus stop (or from the Olympic) to the stadium. Hundreds of sidewalk cracks (present not by design) and street signs that read FRISBY and VENABLE were typical reminders that I was headed for enjoyment at this beloved sanctuary.

I suppose these thoughts will have to suffice while Memorial Stadium lives on in my own mind. I'm not one for demolitions and being on-site to retrieve bits and pieces of the property. That's for amateurs (and collectors, I suppose). I know what once stood like a fortress on Thirty-third and Ellerslie.

I'll let that be my reminder.

33

Secure (and most importantly, content) in my work at the offtrack betting facility, I began to steadily seek additional assignments. It was as though the realization of employment opportunities bred a quest for more tasks.

Through an ad in the classified section, I actually landed a second full-time job. It was at *Bowlers Journal*, whose office was on Chicago's Michigan Avenue. Putting to use my communications major from Towson State, I was hired as a writer with occasional feature story assignments—the attraction that lured me in the first place. I wrote some decent stories there. But I found more glamour in booking my editor's baseball bets. He wasn't a very big bettor, so that's why I decided to play the "house" role. He was a pretty good authority on baseball, though, and I usually had to pay out.

All told, I wasn't long for the *Bowlers Journal* gig. For one, I really wasn't into it; but most of all, the hours, coupled with my shifts at the racetrack, were killing me. I remember the day the whole thing came to a head. I was in my editor's office for an impromptu meeting regarding the upcoming issue and deadlines. It was actually a pretty important little gathering. I do not recall the bullet points whose definitions I was supposed to retain that day, but I do remember dozing off at least three or four times and violently jerking my head up in valiant (but vain) attempts to remain awake. Those are embarrassing reactions. They're not the big production that you think they might look like, but everyone in the room takes notice.

A day or two later, the editor called me in and "suggested" I resign. It was as though he was trying to get me to plead my case, tell him that I'm going to fly straight and produce from that point on. I didn't. I welcomed the easy out he was presenting to me. Who knows, maybe if I did counter with a case in my own defense, he might've fired me anyway. I didn't care. I wanted out.

A few days later, I got a message on my answering machine from him. He wanted to know if it was all right if he kept making baseball bets with me.

My real calling (or opportunity to sate my passion, anyway) came soon thereafter when I was hired on a freelance basis by the Chicago *Daily Southtown*. This was what I wanted: a sports reporting gig. The assignments were for coverage of local high school teams (and an occasional pro assignment—I did a Bulls-Knicks game one Christmas). The topic, for one, was one in which I was as well-versed as I would possibly be in any other realm. I liked this new job. I made new friends.

And new favorites.

As with any other undertaking, I made it into a relationship. While there was nothing halfhearted about my approach to my assignments and new "favorite" teams, these connections were all destined to take a back seat to my bond with Baltimore. But, man, did I have fun. I was quite vocal about my favorite teams over beers with my co-writers and on the printed page (well, as much as the editors would allow with the latter praises). I altered my racetrack schedule to allow for more and more of the lesser-paying newspaper assignments. I was to the point where I kept the bare minimum amount of hours to retain full-time status—and only that many for the sake of keeping my rung on the all-important seniority ladder.

My life consisted of long nights with broken-down horse players, lengthy commutes to high school sporting events (I often made "deals" to accept such assignments in exchange for future games involving "my" teams), and in the late hours, beer and sports wagering at a throwback secret tavern.

And through it all, I counted the days and made all of the appropriate adjustments for two visits a year by the Orioles.

What didn't sit well was my fear of contentment with my location. Looking back—and forward—I'll always be of the mind that adulthood is the single biggest tragedy in life. Responsibilities are part of the package, I understand that and readily comply. But that doesn't mean I have to enjoy it. There are so many little things that add up, things we assume we're required to do and possess simply because of reaching a certain age. For instance, an automobile is an absolute must. I'll begin a rant against motor vehicles and base it on the following: (1) Expense. These things are costly, and they're subject to mechanical breakdown at certain time or mileage intervals. Do you know how to fix them? Because I don't. (2) Danger. There are millions of these things on the road with you whenever you drive. What if someone is drunk? What if you're drunk? What if someone else breaks down? What if you break down? Lengthy traffic jams, that's what. (3) Parking. If you reside anywhere where opportunities for fun exist, sports arenas or any entertainment venues are located, chances are pretty good that the area is well populated. Go find a space. And the next day, go through the same ordeal.

In a perfect world, I wouldn't need a car. I'd work across the street, and all of my friends would live in my neighborhood. Kids have it so good. I mean that with the strongest of convictions.

So while my Orioles sightings were limited to six games per season at both Comiskey Park and Milwaukee's County Stadium, I longed to make a return to Baltimore. At this juncture, I had (in my own mind) done everything and been everywhere I needed to experience. Such were my needs and desires that I was fortunate enough to have discovered what truly makes me happy. A pretty simple existence if you ask me.

But it's all I need.

34

During the 1976 minor league (ages eight to twelve) season at Kennedy Park, we played two regular-season games each against seven different opponents. My team swept the Lions and the Yankees while we split with the Tigers, Cardinals, White Sox, Pirates, and Red Sox. In a three-way tie for first at the end of the regular season, we beat both the Cardinals and Red Sox to gain the No. 1 seed in the playoffs, where we beat the Lions and then lost to the Red Sox.

This information is equal parts uninteresting to the outsider and 100 percent accurate and important to my own life.

If you will please stop running, chasing, and prioritizing in your own busy lives, consider the following: you probably have it completely backward. Allow me to explain.

When the above-mentioned breakdown of wins and losses played out (and that's exactly how it went down, team by team, I assure you), I was eleven years old. Baseball was important to me. I had just discovered it, I loved it, and I have never stopped loving it. At eleven, I found that baseball and the Orioles were the most important things in my life. That hasn't changed. Why should it? Should my career take precedence? Maybe a wife and family of my own?

I recall one time when a woman made me do something I ordinarily would not have. I was no more than five years old, and at the time, I really didn't go out and play with the other kids. Two reasons I distinctly remember were (1) I loved the record player. I would sit in front of it for hours and just play 45s and LPs, rocking back and forth. And (2) I was terrified to walk past the Wilson's house, two doors to the south. From what I remember, Mr. Wilson, an elderly man, was once on the porch and made some kind of face at me. I'm sure his intentions were to draw a laugh, but instead, he scared the shit out of me.

As for the persuasive woman, her name was Fran DaVannon. She was probably in her twenties, and she lived one house past the Wilsons. I was so in love with Fran. She would take me to her house, give me a bowl of cereal, and let me watch her cuckoo clock. So one day, I said to myself (not aloud, of course), "Fuck it, I'm going right past the Wilsons. I've got to see Fran."

People change, and people keep suffering. Technology marches forward, costs rise, and dishonesty is prevalent. And it's only going to worsen. Is this progress? I recall my team's baseball scores from the 1976 season because it meant something to me. It made me appreciate the game. I'm not embarrassed to tell you that I went the entire seasons of 1975 (minor league) and 1978 (PONY League) with a batting average of .000, not even hitting so much as a fair ball in the former campaign. I sucked and was inspired to get better. I did. Not very much, but as good as I was going to get. There is no such incentive for kids today. They use continuous lineups of about fourteen batters, coaches pitch in place of rival kids, and score isn't even kept in many cases. Adults have put these new standards into place. Adults are retarded. They ruin everything they touch. Kids are the real magic. Adults should learn from kids, but they don't.

A child will throw a fit and forget about it the next day. A child harbors no anger, just wakes up the next day and tries to decide what the fun is going to be. Adults, on the other hand, will hold a grudge for years, usually over something that has become too clouded to cite its origin with any accuracy. Kids tell you exactly what they feel and exactly what they see. Adults lie about everything.

The saddest thing of all is that kids turn into adults.

There must be another route.

35

Seeking, in earnest, life in Baltimore had one unattainable premise: employment. I'll go to great lengths not to convey a defeatist attitude, but at times, there's no way around it (there I go again). In my defense, at the approximate time that this dire need to reside in Baltimore arose, I will mention that the Internet was still a luxury of the future. I guess that this wasn't really an entirely valid excuse because other people managed to find employment and relocate back then, but it had to be tons tougher.

What I did have going for me was a refusal to let my spirit be dampened. I kept in touch with as many college friends as I could, and through that network came an excuse to return—even if only for a wedding that took place while the Orioles were out of town (ironically, in Milwaukee).

Eternally grateful that Peg Flynn deemed me friend enough to take part in her wedding celebration, I devised an itinerary that centered on the Orioles. The fact that the O's were on the road during my scheduled stay in Baltimore was not a dilemma which I could not reshape. If they had to travel, so would I.

The simple arrangement had me drive from Chicago to Columbia, Maryland, attend Peg's wedding (at which I made a basket catch of her garter), and retire to my room at the site of the reception. The following day, I mixed the past with the present, linking them as tightly as I possibly could. I drove to a vacant Camden Yards for my first-ever visit. As advertised, it was gorgeous. Not tug-at-the-heart-strings gorgeous, no, *that* was Memorial Stadium, an edifice with the decided advantage of a glorious history and memories.

Anxious to experience my reaction to a side-by-side comparison of the two venues, I made that test possible (as quickly as I could) by driving north to the Waverly neighborhood. There I found Memorial Stadium, standing in its assigned spot as if waiting to host another Orioles game—like the entire move to Camden Yards was indefinite, a rumor.

Elsewhere in that beloved neighborhood of a billion stories, I hit my usual spots but found that inevitable change was well underway. For starters, the former Olympic Lounge was no longer. The structure remained, but the establishment once ran by Phil was now void of the pool table that had once been the center of the universe. Gone, too, were all of the familiar faces. Lori, with her doe eyes and truck driver vocabulary, was no longer standing behind the bar, hair pulled back, and beer at the ready.

I didn't ever bother to order a drink. I just turned around and headed to the corner and hoped for more familiar sights at the Stadium Lounge. It wasn't that I was grief-stricken or upset that *my* Olympic Lounge had disappeared. Its replacement just wasn't my kind of bar.

Now the Stadium Lounge, at least that place still had the Oriole bird painted on the outside wall (and still does). Once inside, I found it packed with locals, a few of them familiar, but from years prior and from other establishments. And it was for those reasons that I was (almost) inclined to approach them and exclaim, "Hey, you're the one who I always used to see at . . ." Perhaps it's just me, but I perceive this approach as a major flaw in the human condition. Why is it that we can see someone on almost a daily basis—in a work setting or on public transportation for a daily commute—even if we're somewhat attracted to them, we'll never speak up during those daily grinds. But the moment we're suddenly face-to-face on previously uncommon foreign ground, our vocal chords and courage are miraculously well. Happens all the time.

Back to the Stadium Lounge. Now I was *not* attracted in the least to any of these particular (visual only) blasts from my Baltimore past. But I must admit that the urge to see if they might remember me stirred, only for a moment, though. Unlike my previous stop, the Stadium Lounge did not make me feel the slightest bit unwelcome. There was, however, a downright tragic element in the air that hastened the consumption of my beer, transforming it from possibly refreshing to headache inducing. Sometime between my last visit and this one, the Maryland Lottery had introduced Keno to what seemed to be the majority of the bars in the state. So roughly every three minutes, a new game played out on a live television feed. I needn't tell you that this attracted the elderly and pretty much anyone receiving a steady government check. Their incomes were fixed, all right. The Keno house/saloon combination seemed to run smoothly enough, but after a period of time, people ran out of money, and that's where the panhandling inevitably began. I saw it every day at the offtrack betting facility and was painfully aware of the incredibly steep odds these losers were facing. First and foremost, the Keno concept is deceptive. Oh, they're picking twenty numbers, and all you need to do is match a few. That's where most people stop doing the math, which tells us there are eighty possible numbers from which to choose.

If the bettor wants to at least double the unlikelihood of winning (which I swear, more times than not that he or she does), throw in the combination of alcohol and gambling and you've got an incredible advantage for the house.

I had somewhere else to go. So I went.

While none of these stops—Columbia, Camden Yards, Waverly, and its saloons—had been chance visits, nor was my next destination. En route to Chicago, I had one last attraction on my schedule: Cleveland's Municipal Stadium. Exactly the halfway point of the trek between Baltimore and Chicago, Cleveland afforded me an opportunity to not only see the Orioles, but also to experience one of baseball's most historic venues—at which I would be attending the ninth-to-last Major League game before it gave way to Jacobs Field.

Having checked out of my Motel 6 room just before noon, I had roughly six hours to kill before I could settle in at Municipal Stadium. Downtown Cleveland was, at that point, undergoing a renaissance of sorts; and I was able to find a new movie theater. Cinema, above perhaps all else, is the ideal way to kill time. As the lone patron for *Money for Nothing*, I was given a "private screening" of the film, and then I headed to the cavernous building that was Municipal Stadium.

There was nothing remarkable about it. Additionally, the Indians and I had no history other than I've always thought of them as less than mediocre and, as a result, annually dangerous when you had to face them with a playoff berth on the line—a playoff berth for which only your team was eligible.

The place was huge. I could see where it could draw better than thirty thousand and still look empty. Whatever dim mathematical hopes the O's may have had grew even cloudier that night. Cleveland came from behind in a game whose biggest highlight was a guy in a green sweater running onto the field and making his way around the bases. Strange, nobody tried to stop him. Perhaps it was because his planned route was obvious, but I still figured on somebody pretending to be a hero by taking the guy down, say, between second and third.

Maybe idle behavior and patience really was the best way to handle it. Maybe an unplanned interruption in this guy's "act" would have resulted in an impromptu alternate route. Who knows?

And who cares.

36

The more familiar I become with Baltimore, the more voluminous my memory storage becomes. While their accumulation is limited to well-planned and repetitive transports, walks through downtown streets, and mostly, evenings spent in saloons, these nuggets vary from human form to random physical objects to scenes that play out to showcase poignant symbolism, imitating life, mocking experience.

My romantic taste steers me back to destinations past, like the Club Charles. There, circa 1987, I had come to know that I would always return to Baltimore. Having rented an apartment on Calvert Street, near Johns Hopkins, I subsequently strayed from the campus scene in Towson. My earliest recollection of the Club Charles is marked by an introduction to what photographic evidence tells me was a pimp and two of his alluring prostitutes. I can tell just by one glance at two or three images from that night that I had way too much to drink. Still, each likeness reminds me that it must have been the type of night on which anything could have happened. The unusual company I kept was (visually) accepting of my social (and drunken) advances. All in good fun, mind you.

So here I sit, some twenty years later, as a visitor, not a resident. In a wishful and trite anticipation, I remotely wait for those same characters to walk in for an unplanned reunion. In a perfect world, I'd have never left Baltimore. But in the Master's plan, the grand scheme, I am back in town for an Orioles weekend, sitting in Club Charles, watching traffic in the mirror behind the bar. It appears as though it is approaching me with brake lights sequentially flashing, car by car.

The reality, of course, is that their stops are only temporary.

And they're headed north on Charles Street, not south as it appears in the mirror.

37

We all harbor good ideas and noble intentions. The lion's share of these never come to fruition for whatever reason. Some of us get married, and lifelong plans are resultantly altered. Some then have children, and any new ventures become more difficult, still. Whatever our life situations, for those of us who follow baseball, the game itself—the daily schedule, pitching rotations, and batting orders—mirrors any semblance of organization in life.

The weekend arrives, and a new series begins. It usually ends on Sunday as we, too, prepare to report to work the next day for the beginning of another week. This continues. Sometimes it's fun, other times, not so much. "Projects" or visits to certain friends or relatives are put off until after baseball season.

What do we do without it?

I spent two summers without it (or sizable portions of those summers, anyway): 1981 and 1994. And I still cannot remember what I did. Calendar years quickly come to mind with the playing of certain songs or the mention of specific baseball events. Nothing else serves me nearly as well in this categorizing.

I can convey a thousand different times that I don't understand high finance, labor laws, unions, and negotiations in the very least. I'm not proud of that, but I'm not ashamed of it, either. And I needn't pretend that I grasp the specifics of the 1994 baseball strike. I can tell you, however, that it was entirely greed-based and equal parts sad and utterly shameful. Basically, neither party gave a shit about the fans. That is the shameful element. The on-field product had become (and continues to, in my opinion) increasingly worse; and very gradually, we have all lost sight of how the game was once played. Lost sight for good, I'm afraid.

The sad aspect of the 1994 strike—and any strike that may follow—is that like a lot of other fans, I'm going to welcome the game back the moment the dispute (whose specifics I'll never understand) is settled. Does that make me a sap? If you say so. But I'll liken it to parenthood. I've seen a lot of mothers and fathers let their kids get away with murder as if nothing had ever happened. And I'm talking about some repetitive garbage that, after the second or third time, I'd definitely drive the kid to most crowded New York City street, open the car door, and leave him/her there and never come back.

I guess that's why I'll never be a parent.

38

Am I so shallow that I cannot function in the absence of baseball? Not really, although I can't recall what I did during those play stoppages. I'm assuming that in 1981, I simply continued in my neighborhood lob league endeavors—the only baseball contests that saw me post a batting average of higher than .200. In '94, area saloons probably got my business a little more. I'm sure there was no great bout with depression.

I just would have preferred that the games had gone on.

And when they finally did report back to the diamond in 1995, it was like Christmas Day all over again, or like my best friend had just been released from a correctional facility that had wrongfully held him for a crime committed by someone else.

In short, all was right and good in the world. Baseball was back, and I was willing to forget that any players' strike had ever occurred. This was the time to get to Camden Yards—to show that I was indeed ready to welcome back this grand game with open arms.

Putting into motion the plan to again witness baseball in Baltimore—where I believe it was meant to be played—I pulled into Midway Airport to purchase an airline ticket, a not-so-difficult task in the days before Internet and 9/11. Southwest had a "Friends Fly Free" promotion going. Unaware that I was going to be the recipient of two tickets, I had to think quickly, not at all accustomed to such departures from solo journeys. For starters, I had no idea who I wanted to join me. Actually, I preferred to go alone.

But here's this free ticket.

Well, I guess there's Julie. I really didn't know Julie. She was the receptionist at the chiropractor's office I had been visiting. Each visit, she'd sign me in and direct me to one of three rooms where she'd arrive about five minutes later and wrap some type of compression sleeve around my lower back. Each time, I purposely reported to the wrong room, hiding behind the door, under the gurney—drawing a laugh from Julie.

I had never met her before, but I recognized the name and knew that I had gone to grade school with her older sister.

So maybe Julie would like to see Camden Yards, too? Didn't cost me anything to ask, so I put her name down on the companion ticket and mailed it to her house with a note to explain that she needn't feel obligated, as it was a free ticket, and well, if she wasn't doing anything that day . . .

So the moment of truth was at hand some three weeks later as I stood in line to board what was to be the first of many, many flights to Baltimore. And up walked Julie. It was a moment I'll always savor. Here's this girl, a virtual stranger in whose presence I had spent maybe a combined six minutes' time, and we're going to Baltimore together to see a baseball game, visit the busy downtown bars, and fly back the next day.

The Texas Rangers were in town that night. Leo Gomez homered for the Orioles, who won in walk-off fashion in the tenth inning. The trip went as I hoped—actually, beyond. Suddenly, with one new experience, I was enamored to unprecedented heights. Having experienced fleeting and all-too-abbreviated courtships with girls of all types, neighborhoods, and social backgrounds, I was figuratively walloped with the uncompromising truth of what love meant. To fall helplessly for something, leave for the better part of seven years, and return only to be swept by those same chills and heart-gripping visual effects—this was the faithful companion that had dutifully maintained its wondrous aura in my absence. This was the institution to which I now had no alternative but to return. The Baltimore Orioles. The city of Baltimore.

The fire never flickers.

39

Julie and I remained friends. I think we went fishing one day. We also climbed to the roof of my old kindergarten building one drunken night. Ultimately, we went separate ways. That's not to say that I didn't care for Julie. I liked her quite a bit. But shortly thereafter, she became a police officer, and her abrupt change in personality was not only unexpected, but also hugely disappointing. I guess in this matter, "unexpected" and "disappointing" are directly linked as it's not too often that personality traits do a complete about-face—not in adulthood, anyway.

Of course, Julie's metamorphosis took shape long after our Baltimore excursion. But it was Baltimore, not Julie or any other acquaintance, that had now wrested my attention, repeatedly beckoning and asking, "Why did you leave?" and "When are you coming back?"

I found what qualified as a "good" reason to return to Baltimore just weeks after my initial trip to Camden Yards. September approached, and so did Cal Ripken, Jr.'s date with baseball immortality: a streak of 2,131 consecutive games played.

I was fully aware that I had absolutely no chance of obtaining a ticket. But I booked a flight and a hotel room, anyway. I knew the streets of Baltimore were going to be decorated with swarms of fans who didn't have tickets, like myself, but would play a part in the celebration, the tribute, simply by show of support. The city and its asymmetrical geographical dimensions had no way of containing the collective pride that had swelled in anticipation of the state's favorite son surpassing a standard that nobody had previously fathomed would fall.

I had followed the club from the onset of the improbable streak and naturally was impressed by it. But this achievement meant so much more to me. Cal Ripken was the last link to the glory days, to seasons during which fans rightfully expected victory each night no matter the opponent or precipice. When I got to college, I was starting a new life and social coming out. I was young then. So was Cal. The object of every Baltimore girl's affection, this tall specimen had bushy hair and those trademark blue eyes. And oh, could he play. Together with Eddie, Roenicke, and the rest of the potent bats, he protected Baltimore's legacy as the best baseball city in the world. And he did it with humility and class that never waned.

I'll always remember Game 3 of the 1983 ALCS. Early on, Mike Flanagan hit White Sox rookie Ron Kittle and drew the ire of the home team. With retaliation in order, Sox pitcher Richard Dotson promptly hit Ripken, leading off the very next inning. Only a few likenesses have remained in my mind and maintained the same vivid quality of the picture that was planted that evening. It's an image of Ripken, having failed to get out of the way of a pitch aimed directly at him, shrugging off the sting (if any), and looking back at Dotson with the grin of a veteran with three times his experience. From accounts I've heard over the years (with most matching, blow by blow), Ripken said to Dotson, "Is that all ya got?" as he jogged to first base. This was the early stage of Tony LaRussa's managerial career, and long before he was to secure World Series wins in both leagues, he didn't handle every situation with the tact required for a skipper of his stature and (now) impressive qualifications. For starters, Flanagan hit Kittle with what I believe was a 3-2 pitch. Regardless of the count, Kittle was an all-or-nothing hitter from the word "go." I never saw him make an adjustment at the plate. All or nothing—and at this particular juncture, it was nothing. Which begs the question: why not let a sleeping dog lie? Flanagan wasn't throwing at anyone, much less, Kittle.

So Ripken's comment struck a chord with Dotson, who proceeded to throw at Eddie Murray. The normally dormant Murray was, of course, suddenly very vocal. The potential of "ugly" (and not "winnin' ugly") loomed large.

And Dotson fell apart.

The streak, as I said, is remarkably impressive. But I flew to Baltimore with no prospects for a game ticket on September 6, 1995, to merely be present to honor (albeit from outside the medieval facade that was the Camden Yards warehouse) a man who embodied the Oriole tradition and, yes, work ethic. I didn't need a ticket. I made purchases from on-site vendors, snatched a free T-shirt, and enjoyed proud memories of the whole day. This was yet another influential moment in the imbued city to which I just had to return. Forever.

40

The excitement over Ripken's feat and my first two (well, one and a half) visits to games at Camden Yards did not, unfortunately, translate to a postseason berth for Baltimore in 1995.

But 1996 would be different. I prepared to begin, in earnest, to formulate a plan to make Baltimore my permanent residence. Years later, I know that intent and reality are galaxies apart.

As for my determination back in 1996, it was steadfast and unwavering. But like anything designed to plow through would-be obstacles, my mind-set, no matter how strong, was no match for fate.

Nothing, not even the most sturdy pillar, can overcome fate.

41

My freelance gig with the Chicago *Daily Southtown* played a sizable role in what has been, without question, the most significant day of my life. Significant, in this case, not in terms of an achievement, revelation, or chance meeting, but significant in that it abruptly altered the course of my existence, thoughts, mind-sets, and reactions regarding everything that has transpired from that fateful day forward.

Like anything else that occurs, the events on this day took form as one piece after another fell into place. None of the building blocks were directly responsible for what was about to happen. Timing and happenstance, as they always do, took over.

Seeking more and more newspaper assignments, I had migrated to Lemont, Illinois, a suburb about fifteen miles southwest of Chicago. Comprised of churches and bars, Lemont had captured me under the guise of a quaint little town that eventually wore thin and became transparent to reveal a drug-decayed community with a stagnant mind-set—for its failed businesses and acceptance of its undesirables, alike.

I loved it at first. Everything about it: my studio apartment above the drug store, my Murphy bed, the drinking establishment with a vintage neon Blatz sign, the high school and its underdog sports teams—I loved it all.

On Saturday, March 9, 1996, I strolled into a bar in downtown Lemont and spotted my landlord's niece. I didn't really know her, but I did know that she was not of legal drinking age and friendly enough to welcome me that night as if to seal my desired status as a "local," even if I had been in town only a few short weeks.

Running into her is, to this day, a blur at best. As for the rest of that night, the following morning, and the weeks that followed, those are lost forever.

I have no idea what happened. Others, unfortunately, have recalled the events with frightening clarity.

But I'll never know for sure what happened.

42

Had I been given the task of phoning my mother that morning, I'm positive that I could have eased into the facts so as not to cause alarm or unrest of any kind.

Have you ever heard the tale of the man who plots with another to rescue him from a would-be grave, only to learn that his accomplice himself has been buried? Well, on March 10, 1996, that was me. I was rendered inoperative that morning, so someone else had to call my mom and induce a frantic state.

Relayed to me weeks later when I finally came to was that the message that morning was one that summoned my immediate family to Christ Hospital.

In the backseat for a ride I'll never recall, I caught the brunt of the impact as the driver veered off a two-lane highway and hit a utility pole at about seventy miles per hour. My right leg was broken, my pelvis was shattered, there were pieces of glass lodged into my face and eyelid. And my skull was fractured.

Surveying the wreckage, the Lemont fire department called for a helicopter to airlift me to the nearest shock trauma center. In the days that followed, I remained unconscious and was administered last rites.

I would spend fifty-one days in Christ Hospital, then remained bedridden for an additional two months as physicians awaited healing of both my pelvis, which was secured by metallic fixators that protruded from my hips and stomach—and my leg, which was adorned with equally unattractive hardware.

Speech therapy and physical therapy unveiled a new side of me. In short, I was pissed off and let everyone know it.

I'm not haunted in the least by whatever memories I have of that trying period. But I don't appreciate the repeated tales of my behavior. Whatever medication I was given had obvious adverse effects as it would with anyone who was so prescribed. So when I screamed at you to fuck off or when I ripped off my bedsheets and gown, unveiling my goods in the process, it was because my mind and actions were not my own. I'm sure you remember it all, but I don't remember any of it. It literally wasn't me. So I don't need to hear about it.

I won't contend for one second that I resent anyone who reminds me of these drug-induced actions. I had incredible support throughout a lengthy recovery. For that, I am thankful and will not forget. But I (literally) walked away from it all with the sense, tact, and discipline to withhold unpleasant information from those for whom I care. Taverns are the perfect arenas in which to practice this. That's really what I learned from the whole ordeal. When a friend gets drunk, loud, and stupid (within the limits of good taste), if he doesn't recall the "damage" he may have done the night before, I'll interrupt with, "You were fine. Shit, I thought I had way more than you."

A neighbor of mine was screaming at his teenage son one night. He got so angry that he punched a hole in his wall. I heard the whole thing; but that night, as we downed a bucket of beers in downtown Lemont, I denied hearing him at all, claiming that I was playing canasta on the Internet and didn't hear a goddamn thing.

When you're not in control, you don't want to be observed. When you regain control, you don't need to hear of your performance while your mind was not your own.

We've all been there, so turn the page.

43

The clouds eventually lifted. It had to be mid-April because the Orioles won eleven of their first thirteen games, and I don't remember a thing about it. To this day, I still have a folder filled with "assignments" I completed in various therapeutic sessions. These were handwritten compositions that made no sense from start to finish. Judging by the content, it's quite clear that my cognitive abilities were limited to maybe a minute. Maybe less. After the first line or two, I began adding extra letters, straying from the lines on the page, and just ceasing to make any sense at all.

My first clear memory was of a letter I received. Perhaps it's selective memory or maybe it's entirely coincidental that the letter arrived the moment I got my act together. But the letter had Orioles content.

It was from Tony, the elderly "assistant" at the gambling bar I frequented. Basically, Tony stood at the end of the bar, showed you the odds, and wrote your wager "receipt" when you paid him. He was nothing short of a miserable prick—to everyone but me. About ten years prior, Tony was basically a vagrant alcoholic. He hung out at a bar called "Clown's Alley" (or perhaps on the sidewalk in front of it). One day, someone decided to give him a chance and hired him in this "cashier" capacity. It worked. Tony was clean. Off the bottle. Just miserable.

His message was heartfelt. That's why I still have it. He wrote: "Your Orioles are really doing great," with hand-drawn lines on an otherwise blank sheet placed probably to help offset delirium tremors. Whatever the case, I got a get-well wish and an update on my Orioles from a guy who was more likely to cash a winning lotto ticket than to crack a smile.

People are awfully good. It's just a matter of noticing it.

44

On crutches and regaining my strength all summer, I was limited to one live Orioles contest at Comiskey Park. My attention, however, was quicker to revert to peak form. All was well at home, too. It was clear that—save for some cosmetic flaws and a leg that would require attention and self-administered therapy for the rest of my life (actually, minor inconveniences considering my status at the scene of the accident)—I had escaped any real damage and had bounced back surprisingly well. A baseball-themed gala was in order in mid-September as my younger brother got married to a neighborhood girl and threw the reception at Comiskey Park. While I might have questioned the monetary cost of a venue that, after a few hours, would be forever sealed to that night's invitees, I'll admit that it was an impressive and memorable event. I was the best man, and shortly after we all arrived to the ballpark (the White Sox were in Oakland that night), the principals of the wedding party were summoned down to the field to pose for photographs. Defiant at first, I delayed the shoot by standing near the visitors' dugout, refusing to report to the Chicago bench. The photographer immediately refused my request and ordered me over to join the compliant subjects.

I was only kidding. Of course, I would have preferred the visitors' dugout, but I didn't expect my request to be granted as I was never a welcome patron at that ball park.

45

Less than two weeks after gaining a new family member, a return to normalcy was mirrored by what was to be the Orioles' first successful bid for a postseason berth in thirteen years. Like so many things lately, this, too was interrupted.

This time, I got the phone call.

I was in my apartment on a Sunday morning and my brother, Pete—he of newlywed status—called and said, "Come out here, something happened to Ricky." I hung up the phone and, strangely, began scrubbing my floor, positive that it was the right thing to do at that instant. I hadn't asked Pete for a single detail. He said his one sentence, and I answered affirmatively and hung up the phone.

Sight unseen, story untold, I knew for absolute certain that my brother Rick was dead.

They were all at my sister's house—gathered on the front steps, in the driveway, on the sidewalk. From my car, I made eye contact with them, two or three of them, as I parked. I didn't need confirmation. My brother's tone during his phone call and, now, these blank stares told me all I needed to know. In summary, Rick never woke up that morning. That's all I ever got out of it and all I ever needed to get out of it.

The circumstances surrounding what turned out to be our last few meetings were out of the ordinary—most definitely not taken from a script that defined a childhood relationship marked by oppression on his part and fear and resultant submission in my own role. So we didn't always get along. That, of course, is inherent to growing up. All brothers fight at some time. I'd be worried if they didn't. Turns out, Rick and his wife drove out to see me in the hours before my automobile accident. I thought it rather unusual that *he* took the initiative to travel thirteen miles to come visit *me*. But he did, and though I'll never recall what happened that night, I can only assume that it was a pleasant exchange between Rick and me.

In the months following the accident, Rick borrowed $35 from me one night. Not sure if he'd remember or ever intend to repay me, I had written it off. But there he was, summoning me as I sped down the stairs of my grandmother's apartment building. It was a weeknight, and I had just returned to my job at the offtrack betting facility. On the way home, I'd stop at about the halfway mark and play canasta with my grandmother—sometimes marathon sessions. That woman seldom, if ever, went to sleep before 2:00 a.m. That's just how she was.

So after one of those battles of "melding" and catching the opponent with his/her red threes, I exited and heard my name called. A cousin of mine lived on the second floor and that's where Rick was with the door open. I'll always remember he was smiling when I changed directions and walked in toward him. He reached in his pocket and pulled out the money he owed me.

"Here's your money, Dr. Spock."

For years, he called me by that name. Initially, it was a derisive moniker as I reminded him of *Star Trek*'s "Mr. Spock." So unbeknownst to Rick, he continually called me by the famed pediatrician's title. Whatever his intentions, I never minded being called by that name because one certainty was that whenever he called me "Dr. Spock," we were getting along at the time. I thought nothing of it then, but recalling that brief meeting now, I have to say that it was an atypical Ricky encounter.

I thanked him and went on my way. I don't think I was two blocks away before I had counted the money and discovered thirty-four dollars instead of thirty-five.

It was the last time I ever saw him.

I will forever be assured of only one thing: that I will never understand what binds us. I don't believe anyone knows. I quickly went back to my daily routine with nary a glitch after Rick's passing. I've always handled death in that fashion. One reality sunk in immediately, though: I thought to myself that there are people I would miss more than I do Rick, but the logic there is that I've always been much, much closer to these people. Regarding these "close" relatives and friends, I'd remember so many little nuances and tendencies that with Rick I don't remember because I never really learned. That's as much Rick's fault as it is mine. But regardless, the cold reality is that now I'll never get a chance, not one, to find out what he was all about. I really have no idea.

We're all just hanging by a thread. We need to define ourselves and play our parts.

You cannot turn it off and walk away.

—Basia Trzetrzelewska

46

Still somewhat numbed by the recent turn of events (actually, by what they had done to my mother), I continued forward the only way I knew how: by following the Orioles. I cannot render myself reticent and not admit that baseball was still just as important to me in the wake of tragedy.

This is the very nature of the game. Unlike other sports or entertainment outlets, baseball is scheduled *every* day. There's no time to mull over a loss that could cripple, say, a football team. In baseball, you're back out there the next night, so you'd better come to play. There's no idle time which would be ideal for lamenting over personal setbacks. Baseball gives you the easy option to forget about everything and let its every last element pervade your "real" existence.

Baseball—the drug, the vice, the institution—wasn't going away. And as I grasped for truths in the fall of 1996, the Orioles were in the heat of a pennant race.

47

The charge was marred, sadly, by an on-field incident in Toronto.

Talk to virtually any baseball fan—or anyone else who remembers the Roberto Alomar spitting incident—and they'll convey their disgust with Alomar and his actions.

I cannot be so quick to condemn.

First and foremost, too many people dismiss the premise that there are two sides to every story. Anyone who makes the effort to confirm that might read accounts, as I did, that umpire John Hirschbeck allegedly called Alomar a "spic motherfucker." Anger over a horrible call (and it was) on Strike 3 is one thing, but if the punch-out is punctuated with an ethnic slur like "spic motherfucker," somebody's going to erupt—even more so in the intense heat of a game with playoff implications.

Public opinion remains that Alomar is a disgrace.

My opinion is that an incident that took all of approximately thirty seconds cost a great second baseman any chance at a future date in Cooperstown. And the shameful aspect switched sides—without investigation of any sort—a couple of weeks later in the ALCS. I cite, of course, Derek Jeter's game-tying would-be fly out that one Jeffrey Maier altered the course of to touch off what I sincerely believe to be a conspiracy against the Orioles that suppresses the franchise to this very day.

I cannot and will not dismiss Alomar's incident and Rich Garcia's blown call as separate events. I believe the umpires to be a strong unit with strong ties and power. And I believe that ever since the Alomar incident, they've been on a mission to stick it right up Baltimore's ass.

This is a ball whose very trajectory would have rendered it a long out. The killer, however, is that there were two outfield umpires present that night. Are you going to tell me that neither one of them saw what that little fucker did? The rules, in fine print on the reverse of many tickets, clearly state that a fan who interferes with a ball in play is subject to ejection. The very next day, Jeffrey Maier was "upgraded" to a box seat as a "reward" for his interference.

This is a twelve-year-old kid. I'm guessing that his intention was solely to secure a baseball as a souvenir of his day in the Yankee Stadium bleachers rather than to interfere with Tony Tarasco and the Baltimore Orioles. I only called him a fucker because of the smile on his face in the moments that followed. And the Yankees are sending the wrong message by treating him like a king the next day.

He broke the rules and got away with it.

I'm disgusted with Yankee fans to begin with. They are without rival in terms of rude and ignorant behavior. If you're brave enough to enter Yankee Stadium wearing the opposing team's apparel, they'll spit on you, throw beer in your face, and shout unspeakable obscenities. There's just no place for that kind of behavior in baseball. The saddest aspect of it is that names like "Ruth," "Gehrig," and "Huggins" command respect. But the collective unruly behavior of the team's current fans make the Yankees the biggest disgrace in the game.

48

At what point, if any, have you become so involved that your thoughts and those of your idols are identical?

God, I hope such a mind-set is nonsense. But as I began to envision a once-impenetrable Orioles armor now susceptible to the blows of American League opponents—blows that used to just glance off in a harmless direction—I wondered if confidence was shaken in this, a crew of performers who had never played in a lineup with Singleton, Murray, and DeCinces. Additionally, as I grew older than virtually every player on the Orioles roster (for keeps now), what I lacked in playing experience I made up for by having endured thousands of conceivable ways to lose. If I feared the worst, did they, too?

One thing of which I am certain is that while triumph translates to success, it's not the only avenue. Without coming right out with some bullshit hackneyed phrase like "winning isn't everything," I have somehow arrived at this realization.

Since the Orioles were felled by Cleveland in the 1997 ALCS, they have not enjoyed a winning season. Still, year by year, I have followed them more and more closely. It's not out of a sense of obligation but rather a part of my life that's the absolute top priority. So much has changed. And so much has remained the same. Years from now, I'll remember Geronimo Gil the same way as I do Andres Mora. A backup catcher during the recent lean years, Gil was usually a day game-after-night game starter whose abilities warranted that status. Mora, on the other hand was, by all accounts, a pet project of Weaver, who loved the long ball and saw that this kid was clearing the fences in Mexico at an alarming rate. Listening to out-of-state broadcasts as a teen, I remember sporadic pinch-hitting appearances by Mora—all of which resulted in a strikeout.

For some reason, I kept waiting for both of them, Mora and Gil, to become superstars. In a perfect world, all of my Orioles are superstars. Without personal partnership or parenting experience, I suppose I can only assume that the Orioles are the closest thing to an immediate family that I'll ever know. I see it this way: given the choice of boarding a passenger train and, by chance, finding myself sitting next to a long-lost friend/former coworker from my neighborhood or grade school—or finding that the nearby passenger was, say, Geronimo Gil or Andres Mora—I'd opt for the latter every time.

With accurate foresight, I can tell you that any conversation with a grade school contemporary would be strained and uncomfortable (for me, at least). The train couldn't get to its destination fast enough. In fact, I'd probably get up a few miles early and declare, "Well, this is my stop, nice seeing you. Tell everyone I said hello."

If even the most obscure of Oriole players was in my presence, I'd have questions at the ready, sort of a game of "Who remembers more about your career: you or me?" I'm smiling just thinking about it—me asking Andres Mora what it was like to play for Weaver. Who was cooler: Murray or Singleton? Did you guys hate the Yankees and Red Sox as much as we do? Wasn't Ron Guidry just a so-so pitcher? What Baltimore bars did you guys go to the most?

I'd go on for hours with Andres Mora and Geronimo Gil. In stark contrast to my impromptu escape from those childhood acquaintances, I'd even *miss* my stop and stay on the train as long as they did.

Even if I don't speak fluent Spanish.

49

I had no premonition whatsoever of this lengthy funk that has grounded my Orioles for what is currently an eleven-year stretch. There are two distinct characteristics of droughts of any significant length.

First and foremost, there are suddenly less of us. By "us," of course, I refer to fans. So I should rephrase that and say that difficult times will weed out the phonies.

Second, memory no longer serves you well. It goes beyond the baseball diamond, too. When there is less for me to remember regarding the Orioles, the same holds true regarding simultaneous events: births, deaths, historical events—none of them concern me. It's like a filter that renders meaningless anything that can't be tied in with the Orioles. It has nothing to do with intent, either. I'm just not going to remember nearly as much in lean times. Not after I had grown so accustomed to watching the best team on the planet.

And for roughly the first eighteen years of my life, the Baltimore Orioles were the best team on the planet. In any sport.

50

I never would have believed that Rafael Palmeiro used steroids.

I abhor cynics and, as reason would have it, try at all costs to avoid playing the role of an incessant doubter. But some six years prior to Palmeiro's demise, experience taught me that careful investigation can uncover the truth—desired or unwanted. Bear with me as I construct my best analogy.

Nearly three years removed from devastating physical injuries, I quit my job at the offtrack betting parlor and began full-time with a local newspaper. Time, however, had not healed at least one of those physical setbacks. A venous stasis ulcer was the nasty result of permanently damaged veins in my right leg. In layman's terms, my leg was fucked up pretty bad. And unlike any of the other lingering flaws incurred in that car wreck, this one hurt.

I was directed (by a woman in a Chicago saloon) to the Wound Care Center at Little Company of Mary Hospital. There, at the very structure in which I came into this world, I met Dr. Farhad Vossoughi. Because of Dr. Vossoughi, I have use of my right leg today.

Disapproving of the care I had up to that point, this man was all business on his mission to preserve my appendage. He opted almost immediately to perform an Apligraf, a surgical procedure akin to your normal skin graft, but "replacing the divot" with a random baby's foreskin rather than with skin from another part of your own body.

After the surgery, I returned for a debriding. Save for the rare flare-up of my sciatic nerve, this was far and away the most intense pain I had ever endured.

If I am ever to witness a torture the likes of—oh, I don't know—a guy getting skinned alive, maybe, I'll shake my head and say to myself, "Man, I wonder what he did to deserve that? Oh well, at least they didn't touch his sciatic nerve or clean out his venous stasis ulcer, lucky prick."

A memory that will always stick with me was Dr. Vossoughi's reaction to my reaction as he tried—as quickly and delicately as possible—to debride my wound. I have a vivid recollection of wincing in pain and gripping the steel rod attached to the bed. Immediately, he looked up at me and said, "I cannot knock you out every time."

In short, Dr. Vossoughi had pretty much dug a hole—a deep one—to rid my leg of infection and debris. While the new cells melded and actual skin took shape and form, I was by no means allowed to put weight on my leg. So from May until November, I was on crutches and antibiotics. During repeated visits to the Wound Care Center, my progress was monitored with digital images. I healed nicely. Slowly, but nicely. At the end of it all, after having covered high school sporting events on crutches through baseball season, the entire football season, and a small portion of the volleyball campaign, I was given my release by Dr. Vossoughi and handed an envelope containing the photos from each stage of my leg's recovery.

I remember looking at my wound as the nurse removed the dressing each visit. I always thought that it never really appeared to be any better. I didn't see how it was going to heal. But Dr. Vossoughi would nod with approval at each sighting. And when I looked at the entire series of photos, I saw an ever-so-gradual improvement that was impossible to detect on any single viewing.

After being hypnotized by Palmeiro's wagging finger during the court hearings, I bought his firm denial as the absolute truth. This guy wasn't the lab experiment that Bonds appears to be. But when the finding was made public in the summer of 2005 that Palmeiro *had*, in fact, used performance-enhancing substances, I sifted through old images of him from his early days with the Chicago Cubs.

He had grown much, much bigger into a completely different physical specimen. It was just very gradual. Too gradual for anyone to notice.

There are many more steroid users than we'll ever suspect. I'm sure of it.

51

Does anyone know when the twenty-first century began? I only ask because everyone I know assumed that date to be January 1, 2000. If my math is correct, 2000 represented the final year of the *twentieth* century and January 1, 2001, marked the beginning of the twenty-first and current century. The media seemed to agree with the incorrect version, catering to the lowest common denominator as it usually does.

My lack of respect for (most of) the news media is deep-seated. I haven't believed in them in years. There are some good ones, but I know that their word isn't the gospel truth that they expect us to believe it is.

Current print media is an absolute disgrace. I'll steer as clear from news and entertainment categories as I am able these days. I've noticed a disturbing pattern in the Comcast Internet page. I recently saw a headline that said something to the effect of "Rivers Against Gay Marriage." I clicked on the link, saw the sponsors' ads (mission accomplished, Comcast), and here's the gist of the story: Joan Rivers was asked about legislature that would legalize gay marriage. In summary, she replied with something witty, explaining that she has so many gay friends that if they're allowed to marry, she'll go broke buying them all gifts.

And Comcast declared "Rivers Against Gay Marriage" in the headline? Are you kidding me?

More recently, still, a Comcast headline read, "Wade Suing Ex for $100 Million." Really? Shit, I didn't even know Dwyane Wade was ever married, let me check this out. Turns out, it was an *ex*-business partner or agent of some sort. What Comcast does is completely unethical. Comcast doesn't care about responsible journalism, all Comcast cares about is the fucking check it gets from the advertiser. Like a lot of things, journalism sucks on many levels now.

As 2000 wore on, I grew steadily disappointed with my own work—not the quality of my work, but with the demands to which I refused to adhere. I got mail and phone calls from one parent after another. Why isn't my little Joey in the paper? Why don't you cover my Tommy's soccer games? Why did you do a feature story on Jason? He's not the whole team, and the other kids resent it.

I knew the answers to those questions. In order: little Joey sucks, and that's why his name doesn't appear in the paper. Little Tommy's soccer games are strictly an avenue for kids who suck at other sports. And Jason *is*, in fact, the whole team. He works much harder than does your punk kid, and I guarantee he's going to achieve much more in life than will your derelict offspring.

I'll always enjoy writing, especially about sports (which, incidentally, I could never play very well, not at all). But as for covering high schools, I'll always remember the final straw. I was covering a girls' high school softball game. A girl had a no-hitter going in what I believe was the last inning. Well, she lost the no-hitter (which would have been her first) on an opposite-field single. She eventually lost the shutout, too (though the game was already well in hand, she didn't have to worry about that). As the girl became unnerved, she started walking people. The catcher was a multisport talent who was subbing for the injured regular catcher. She was also recovering from a torn ACL suffered less than a year earlier on the basketball court. The pitcher's mother—who had repeated run-ins with coaches—started yelling, "It isn't working, Kristin!" to the catcher! This maniac actually believed that it was the catcher's (Kristin's) fault that her daughter suddenly couldn't throw a strike.

There are bad parents, and I know that they're in every town. So it was time for me to look elsewhere for a paycheck.

Crystal Allen, my former pari-mutuel manager, a true friend who had made frequent visits to my hospital room, gladly took me back.

All it took to go back to better pay, better hours, and better friends was one phone call. I was truly the prodigal son. Things were about to get much, much better—one gut instinct after another.

52

Smoke-filled barrooms with angry patrons tearing up their tickets and cussing at the television sets—this was where I truly belonged.

I was none the worse for my absence. I hadn't missed a beat on the Autotote keypads. If you're going to be there for x amount of races, you might as well work fast. Customers appreciate it, and they'll remember you gratuitously for it.

It was shortly after my return to the sin-filled world of gambling that I began repeated returns to Baltimore, each one teasing me, prompting feelings that I truly belonged there, and leaving me begging for a return sojourn. The pattern was one of haunting repetition: I'd land at BWI, take the Light Rail into downtown Baltimore, and get actual chills as soon as I spotted the skyline. This was a feeling even more stirring than the thrill I recall after running down the stairs on Christmas Day, holding the same excitement the tenth time as it did the first. Each person, every structure—I adored them all. And as I boarded that same Light Rail train to return to BWI, the empty feeling was nothing short of unbearable.

The first of these visits was akin to a drug, a mind-altering substance that touches off an addiction from which one cannot recover. Subsequent "fixes" were required more and more frequently, many times while the Orioles weren't even in town. If there was any excuse to go to Baltimore, I was going to find it.

August 15, 2001: Kansas City at Baltimore for 1970s night. I secured my ticket and reported to Camden Yards. My childhood heroes once again graced the field. Rich Dauer was a Royals coach. Scott McGregor, Tippy Martinez, the late Pat Kelly, and Doug DeCinces were on hand in street clothes, so was Boog Powell. Eddie Murray and Ellie Hendricks were O's coaches. And Rick Dempsey delivered an on-field message more poignant than any work, written or spoken, in human history. He recalled the days and nights at Memorial Stadium, the "O-R-I-O-L-E-S" cheer from which there was no escape, and an era during which fans didn't need a scoreboard message to let them know when to make noise. While Dempsey brought that departed spirit back for a few moments, it's a sad fact that those days are gone, maybe forever.

Appropriately, Cal hit a home run, and the Orioles prevailed, 4-3.

What seemed like one fleeting moment at a time, I proceeded to return. My mind was set to get back permanently. For me, this proved an unattainable wish. But I didn't know that I'd ever allow myself to stop trying.

53

I had earned a promotion to pari-mutuel manager, maintaining the Autotote machines and updating the satellite feeds from out-of-town tracks. I was scheduled to open the Romeoville facility one Tuesday morning, and the alarm clock summoned me. I always set the alarm to an AM radio feed, usually a news station that I can't bear listening to, giving me a good reason to leap from my bed and go shut it off.

The news on this particular Tuesday woke me up, all right. Not yet fully coherent, I heard the words "airplane," "World Trade Center," and "Pentagon" and knew immediately that something was way wrong. I reported to work, set things up, and stared at one of the monitors as Delaware Park began its race card. One by one, tracks cancelled their races. Delaware, too (I think they actually ran a race or two—good for them). The world came to a standstill because some radicals who preach nothing but "peace" and "God" decided to attack innocent people.

I'm not well-versed in politics or religion. All I can tell you for sure is that the world is becoming an increasingly bad place and will continue to do so. There is no deterrent for wrong, only measures of prevention that cause more and more inconvenience. Little by little, we have come to actually embrace the garbage we are fed. Graffiti is an example. It is unsightly, and it's a sign of gang activity. Yet I recently saw a tabletop video game in a bar that glorified it. It was a basketball game, a street-themed game in which the player fires three-point attempts at moving targets. In the backdrop, there were brick walls covered with graffiti. Is that what we really want to condone?

If someone is ever caught spray-painting graffiti on a building that doesn't belong to him, he should get his hands chopped off as a penalty.

It's a harsh punishment, I know. But you'd probably never see graffiti again.

54

Despite the utter shock and crippling effect the terrorists brought about on 9/11, they inadvertently altered the Major League schedule so that Cal Ripken, Jr. was allowed to close out his remarkable career at Camden Yards (which, had the season been spared the interruption, would not have happened). Take that, you hateful sons of bitches.

After a patriotic wave swept over the country, complacency soon took over again. We're all guilty in that regard, conveying our heartfelt feelings and loyalty only when something terrible has happened. It wasn't a month removed from the attacks that I boarded a plane for BWI to attend the Towson-Monmouth homecoming football game. Reunited with friends I hadn't seen or talked with in more than a decade, I gradually came to the complete realization that not a thing had changed. This, perhaps more than baseball, was the clear indicator that I absolutely belonged in Baltimore. There are experiments and risky moves, but this was not one of them. It was the equivalent of finding a rock-star parking space on a crowded downtown avenue—just a matter of pulling in and starting your evening off right.

As I surveyed the tailgate scene in the Towson Center parking lot, I had one destination in mind: the Phi Sigma Kappa group. While at Towson, I had joined a different fraternity, but most of my friends were in Phi Sig. I didn't bother to look for my own brothers.

I only wanted to go where I belonged.

55

I purchased a condo in the fall of 2000. For me, this was and will almost certainly always be the biggest commitment I'll ever make. Save for Baltimore and its elements, there is nothing else I'm actually ready for or willing to give my effort and attention. Armed with this knowledge, I consider myself ahead of the game and lucky to be me. I could not fathom a lifelong partner. Damn, I couldn't imagine a two-day mate. I'm not faulting those who decide to pair off and grow a family. It's just absolutely not for me. I want to (and will) come and go as I please without informing or answering to anyone. As for companionship and feelings that sprout from physical attraction, well, I have an answer for that, too: I really don't need it. I don't regard mine as a cynical stance, just realistic. You meet someone, you find that person physically and mentally appealing, and you begin dating.

Hear me out.

There are very, very few experiences, if any, like falling in love. You await her every breath, every glance. If you're lucky, she feels the same about you. Somewhere and someday, you're going to find a flaw. And so will she. Then another flaw, things that piss her off, things that piss you off; and suddenly, it's a world in which you more or less tolerate each other.

Hey, I know we're not perfect, and couples play on each other's positive attributes. Not me, that's all. If I like someone and view her as perfection, I intend to keep it that way. It's not for fear of getting hurt. I just cannot understand why anyone would settle for anything less than perfection. What if someone is to come along and like me? I mean, really like me. She likes my sense of humor, my demeanor, she agrees with my stances (of which she has knowledge, anyway). Do I want to let this girl in to find things she *doesn't* like? Call me silly, but I'm inclined to believe that the natural course of events is that deep down, people want to find fault—and for others to find fault with them.

Count me out of that sector, thank you.

The very nature of my abilities in conversation (or lack thereof) tell me all I need to know about priorities. I can talk at length about a game I remember listening to, or a place in Baltimore, or the night the rain came down in 1984 as a result of Hurricane Diana. As for my views and comments on people, I can piece together nothing more than anecdotal nuggets: a thing someone said, the group he or she hung out with—nothing that would interest the listener.

I knew a girl in college. She was from Ellicott City, and we lived in the same dorm. I think that during my entire tenure at Towson, I spoke with her for an aggregate total of about forty minutes, maybe at a bar or a party on occasion, in the dining hall when I saw her there, or just walking on campus and randomly meeting. I can, with absolute certainty, tell you that each and every "conversation" consisted of some form of joking around. A serious word was never uttered. What I'm left with in terms of memories is her gorgeous face and unforgettable smile (which she wore permanently). That's all.

Why would I ever want to risk spoiling that?

Admittedly, my priorities are selfish. All of them. But I will declare that nobody suffers as a result of my likes, dislikes, and passions. I have always been ready and willing to help friends in need, many times unsolicited. But in everyday circumstances, when all is well with family members and friends, my concerns are for hiring painters to decorate my condo walls with black paint and orange trim, or for finding a store in Oak Forest, Illinois, where I can purchase a neon Oriole bird for all of DuPage County to see every time Baltimore triumphs.

I love women. I absolutely do. It's just that I love the Orioles more. I love to meet girls in bars, go for a meal, take in a movie or concert. It's just not something I wish to make routine. Because if it ever came time to pick and choose, I assure you that the prospect of Melvin Mora extending his hitting streak into double digits is and always will be a far bigger priority to me than will your niece's first communion. I also want (need) the option of waking up at nine on Saturday morning and having the option to go right back to sleep for three more hours. I know relationships, so I know that if there's someone in the bed with me on those mornings, she's eventually going to start waking me up to go do stuff.

You say your folks are dying to meet me? I'm flattered.

But they're going to have to wait until football season. And by that time, I doubt we'll still know each other. Sorry.

56

There is no substitute for experience. Force-feeding anyone with your beliefs—no matter how sincere—will always produce the exact opposite of the desired effect.

Holly wasn't a baseball fan. By that, I mean that she didn't have a favorite team and probably didn't care for the game. She did, however, have a sister in Baltimore. Holly would come with me and go to the Orioles-Devil Rays game on the night before the 2002 Preakness. Holly would be crazy about the aesthetically pleasing venue that was Camden Yards and, out of natural instinct, become immediately attached to its tenants.

It didn't quite happen that way. Actually, though she did go with me to Baltimore—unaware of my intention to expose her to that which she couldn't help but love—she was probably bored with it all. The rain delay didn't help. Holly and her sister actually left during the rain delay and headed to the Harbor for drinks. They may or may not have thought it strange that I chose to wait out the rain delay. All told, the trip worked out well as the Orioles won on the strength of a Jeff Conine home run.

My visits to the Charm City were now in full swing, changing only in their frequency. I've gone with a friend now and then and by myself at least thirty times. While the latter arrangement has always allowed for uninterrupted activities and destinations of my own choosing, something repeatedly told me that I should make the effort to bring along a female companion. And to be perfectly honest, the extent of my intentions was to show off "my" baby (Baltimore, not the girl I brought along). With that climate apparent to both of us, things went just fine. Just baseball, a restaurant or two, and maybe a few bars. Good, clean fun. In the words of Earl Weaver: "If you play for one run, that's all you're going to get."

I hope they were impressed, every one of them.

57

Life is just one written test after another. We're presented with choices every day—all kinds of them—and when we look back on it all, that's where we learn. Someone is keeping score, and I can't wait to see mine. I'm not afraid to see my score because while I know I put down some wrong answers, everybody is taking the same tests (just with the questions in different order, that's all).

Think of all the people you've hung out with. You can figure out a few check marks or gold stars right there.

I worked with a guy named Jay at the offtrack betting facility. He lived in Indiana, which was actually very close to the betting parlor's East Side of Chicago address. We'd go out after work sometimes, I don't know, maybe ten or fifteen times in all. He always bragged about his spots in Lansing, Illinois, telling me how he knew everyone and pretty much ran the show. It's only in hindsight that I realize this guy had real delusions of grandeur. He smoked pot quite a bit, and I heard him say he was a dealer with Mafia connections. He was small and scrawny with a beard. I don't think he necessarily had "small man's complex," but he was never shy about telling you how nobody wanted to fuck with him. I could have (and at times wanted to) picked him up and snapped him in two, and I'm not a fighter. In summary, he was pretty much an asshole. But he enjoyed my company and really didn't have any other friend to speak of, so I tolerated him. He'd come into the parlor on his nights off, drunk out of his mind, and make a complete jackass out of himself. And then he'd do the same shit two or three nights later. Just a loser.

We all accept the wrong things or people every now and then. The key is that we never stop believing that it's our best possible situation and that we should try to make it work. We'll all wake up, sometimes quickly and sometimes more deliberately. But through trial and error, we'll all get to a better situation. Hopefully.

"As we go along . . ."

I enjoy The Call, a late-1980s California-based band fronted by one Michael Been. The aforementioned lyrics can be heard at the opening of "I Still Believe." And don't worry, I'm not going to proceed with some bullshit conveying that is the song that defines me. No, when I hear that song, I don't think of its lyrical content. I just like the beat and how it flows, not too fast and not too powerfully.

As we go along, things happen so fast that we don't realize what's good and what's not good until they're distant memories. I've made journeys to countless games with my blind faith in the likes of Glenn Gulliver, Wayne Gross, Kelly Paris, and Eric DuBose, to name a few. They happened to comprise parts of the cast at different intervals in Orioles history. In short, that's all we had to work with, so that's what we accepted. Sure, I can tell you now that those guys (and many others) ultimately proved *not* to be the answer. But at the time, you don't question their potential or ask if you're getting the best possible product. It's baseball, you'll find out soon enough.

Have you ever met a girl in a bar, and on the very first night, she agrees to go home with you? As you climb the stairs and turn the key to your apartment, you don't ask her where this is going to lead because you virtually already have her bra unfastened. Come sunrise or, if things go well, a few sunrises later, it may hit you that you picked the wrong girl.

Well, until Marty Cordova proves to you that he can't stay healthy for more than ten minutes, you're going to claim him as one of your own and go out to see him night after night.

58

I was dead set against Interleague play the moment it was announced. More than ten years later, I'm still vehemently opposed to it. It takes every last drop of magic out of the World Series. It also makes the schedule so unbalanced that nondivision opponents (usually) make only one trip to each opposing city. Worst of all, division games are scheduled more frequently. For Baltimore, that means eighteen games against each rival in the toughest division in baseball.

Even the "never-before" aspect of it never appealed to me. In 2003, the Orioles hosted the Chicago Cubs, marking the first time the two have ever squared off. I don't care that they've been Major League teams for a combined 160-something years. They've never played each other, and there was always a reason—they're in different leagues.

As long as it was going to happen, however, I had to be there. I flew out for the finale of the three-game series. The Cubs had won the first two, and this cursed franchise was *not* one I wanted to sweep us. (Four months later in the NLCS against Florida, the Cubs proved that they are *most definitely* cursed.) The gods would not allow a sweep of the Birds. Rick Helling enjoyed perhaps his finest outing (one of few good ones) in an Orioles uniform, and Melvin Mora extended his hitting streak to twenty-seven games with a home run in his final at bat. This guy was hitting damn close to .400. I had adopted Mora as my favorite as soon as I read about the quintuplets (and saw an image of his gorgeous wife). Mora is all about hard work. All indications are that he's a tough player and an even tougher human being.

Melvin Mora is who I want on my side. There's a reason he's currently the longest-tenured Oriole. I hope he plays until he's sixty.

That was my inaugural Interleague experience. I was happy to witness a victory and Mora's eleventh-hour heroics, but I was not further enticed by the thought of opposite league matchups.

Interleague play is on the unimpressive résumé of Commissioner Selig. Based on his actions, I'd say Selig is the furthest thing from a baseball purist. During his tenure, he has stood by idly while the game has been tarnished perhaps beyond reproach. The wild card, to me, is just the foot in the door. We may see Major League Baseball have a play-off scenario like the NHL and NBA one day. As long as you can field nine players, you're in. I'm of the mind-set that Selig knew how serious the steroids problem was, too. He didn't give a shit. He wanted McGwire and Sosa to hit 150 homers between them. Does that even mean anything to anyone? Here's a sacred record that Ruth held for thirty-four years. Then Roger Maris held it for thirty-seven seasons. And you're telling me that two clowns come along and shatter it with no problem, and everything is legit? I completely disregard any numbers posted by any of those sideshow freaks. The only definitive read I have on Selig is that he either doesn't know about the game and the historical significance of certain things or he doesn't care about the game or he's kind of a coward—or maybe all three.

Interleague play sucks, and it's worn out whatever welcome it may have had. I'm sure we all have attractive cousins. But that doesn't mean we should sleep with them.

59

The state of the game is, at times, a sad one. An unprecedented wave of losing in Baltimore has something to do with it, yes. But the gradual change that I spoke of earlier has produced a negative effect. I'm routinely more amazed by the actions of certain players than I am with any performances, no matter how stellar. And I know I'm justified in my outrage. Justified but powerless.

The Orioles swept visiting Philadelphia in a 1997 Interleague series. At the conclusion, the Oriole bird mascot stood atop the Phils' dugout with a broom, sending the message loud and clear. Phillies third-base coach John Vukovich became irate and even hunted down the mascot in the dressing room forty-five minutes later, declaring in no uncertain terms what he was going to do with the broom and where he was going to shove it.

Really? Were you *that* tough, John? Given the chance, could you really have whooped a mascot? Shit, I'm impressed!

A few weeks after the Orioles-Cubs 2003 Interleague series, I watched the Birds take on the Yankees in a day game in the Bronx. Sidney Ponson was on that day, besting Clemens by a 5-3 count. I became more angry watching that game than I did during any other—including the 1996 ALCS game with that 12-year-old son of a bitch.

During one of his plate appearances, Mora laid down a bunt. He was subsequently hit by a Clemens fastball, prompting the YES network announcers to explain how Clemens "doesn't like" when people bunt on him. So let me get this straight: Roger Clemens is going to endanger the livelihood of a man with infant quintuplets because he tried to bunt? Clemens is going to intentionally induce pain by throwing a fastball directly at a man who is no stranger to pain, having watched his father being shot and killed. And this is excused because Roger Clemens "doesn't like" when people try to bunt on him? This is the same Roger Clemens who picked up the jagged half of Mike Piazza's broken bat and hurled it at Piazza during the 2000 World Series. Can you say "'roid rage?"

Roger Clemens, you're a piece of shit.

I talk baseball to express my love for the game and the Baltimore Orioles. I'm not here to attack players I don't like (and there's a long list of them). But I'll contend that Roger Clemens is a laboratory experiment who needs not look further than the above-mentioned incidents to learn why he'll never have a date to keep in Cooperstown.

I found it curious in Jose Canseco's 2005 book, *Juiced: Wild Times, Rampant 'Roids, Smash Hits, and How Baseball Got Big*, that the author outed his contemporaries from cover to cover but interrupted his venom spewing for an entire page to basically perform fellatio on Clemens. In midstream, Canseco stopped his flow to admire Clemens for being "one of the very few baseball players I know who never cheated on his wife." I just found it to be way out of context, that's all. Canseco reverted to lashing out at those who far outclass him, most prominently, Cal Ripken, Jr. Canseco made absolutely ludicrous hypothetical comparisons to those with histories of questionable conduct (including himself) and Ripken. He cited the incident where former Indians outfielder Albert Belle fired a baseball at a fan in the stands, claiming that if Ripken had done the same, it would have been treated as a joke. He went on to bring up the 2003 incident in which Sammy Sosa's bat broke during a game, only to be exposed as a cork-filled weapon. Had the white ash belonged to Ripken, "there's no way any ump would have made an issue out of it" (according to Canseco). He then made the claim that if a loaded automatic weapon was found in Ripken's vehicle (as one was in Canseco's), police would have backed off with sentiments the likes of "Excuse me, Mr. Ripken, sir."

Hey, Jose: (1) Ripken would never lack the self-control to refrain from firing a ball at a spectator, (2) Ripken wouldn't use a corked bat, and (3) Ripken wouldn't be in possession of a .9-mm automatic pistol.

Nor would he have vanity plates that read, "40-40."

60

Indelible impressions are what they are. They don't require repetition or documentation. You experience something, and it either stays with you or it doesn't.

That being said, the city of Baltimore is character defined. I will go to my final resting place with more memories of Baltimore than I will of any other place. On the northeast corner of St. Paul Street and North Avenue, there's an old, long-since vacated building. Emerging from the very corner of the structure is an old thermometer. Obviously installed along with the building decades ago, this device does not offer a digital reading but, rather, a clock-type indication. Starting at -20 degrees (at 8:00), the readings go upward, clockwise—all the way to 120 degrees—which is at about 4:00.

The thing is still functioning. And I'm quite certain that it accurately reaches that 120-degree reading on some days.

61

Somewhere along the way, I've grown accustomed to losing. I'll never accept losing. I'll never enjoy losing. But there have been days, even weeks, when I couldn't possibly imagine any other outcome.

Maybe another Palmer or Murray will never come along again. Maybe they will. But that first glimpse of what I perceive to be the panacea is what has kept me going for all these years.

Early during the 2004 season, I took my half-hour break from work at the offtrack betting parlor and drove to Burger King. The Orioles were in Chicago that night playing the White Sox. The Sox won. It was either 15-0 or 16-0. I got teased a little bit when I reported back to work. But my reply to all of them was that Baltimore was going to win the next game, 1-0, and the series would be even—despite the colossal run differential.

They got rained out the next night; but the following day, they played a doubleheader, and Baltimore won the opener, 1-0.

My own prediction was not what impressed me that afternoon. The stage that day belonged to one Daniel Cabrera. In his Major League debut, he completely dominated the White Sox. I was convinced that this six-foot-seven stud (I believe he actually grew to six-foot-nine a couple years later) was going to make us all forget about the likes of Mussina, Key, and Erickson.

And I stayed convinced for five long years. Through countless walks, wild pitches, and atrocious defense (Cabrera could absolutely not field his position), all I could see was that debut and a near no-hitter at Yankee Stadium. I fell for it. I'll always love Daniel Cabrera, just like I'll always love Ben McDonald. I recall a game against the Red Sox in which Cabrera (enduring a typically bad outing) balked home a run during the late innings. It was the correct call, he did balk. I think he knew it was the correct call, but at that very moment, every morsel of frustration—the same frustration I had felt while watching this work in progress—caught up to him and he reached a boiling point. He threw the next pitch behind Dustin Pedroia, and the benches emptied.

I certainly wasn't fearful regarding what might happen to Cabrera during a brawl. I don't think any human being in his right mind would dare approach such a monstrous physical specimen. But I genuinely felt sorry for him. I realized as I watched him in all his misdirected rage that he had the physical potential to be the greatest pitcher the game has ever known. But he completely lacked the mental makeup required to survive even the tamest of rallies.

62

I've noticed while driving or walking down Charles Street that people generally don't know what makes them happy. On a recent March afternoon, I was on the Homewood Campus of Johns Hopkins University to take in the season opener for the Blue Jays' baseball squad (simultaneously, the school's highly touted lacrosse team was in action). It was sunny and about seventy degrees—a welcome change from the typical conditions of late winter/early spring. On the main lawn, right off Thirty-third and Charles, there were hundreds of people sitting on blankets, throwing Frisbees, playing catch with baseball gloves. They were enjoying the pleasant weather, true. But you could absolutely sense contentment and tranquility. On this day, everyone was eager to be or become friends. And it was the balmy temperature and sun-drenched surroundings—nothing else—that prompted this euphoria.

Since that day, there have been plenty of afternoons with similar (and even nicer) conditions. But that lawn has been all but empty. Where are they all? Where are their smiles? They had embraced that day and their surroundings so eagerly. Was that their allotment? Could those conditions be conducive to enjoyment of self and acceptance of others only once?

I'm not sure if folks will ever find something or someone and accept it forever.

We make far too many demands.

63

It may sound as trite as the day is long, but networking is a good thing.

Rhiannon, an acquaintance and bartender in Lemont, Illinois, told me of a sports memorabilia auction house for which her mother worked. She suggested that I forward her my résumé and see if a fit was possible. More than three months went by before I received a phone call while on my day shift at the offtrack facility. It was the head writer at Mastro Auctions.

We scheduled an interview, and just days later, they offered me a position. There was a great deal to consider here. At the offtrack parlor, I worked Monday, Tuesday, and Wednesday and had four straight off days. The money was decent (provided I didn't gamble, which I didn't), and on top of that, there was a gentleman who frequented the place named Moses. Appropriately, Moses was nothing short of a Christ figure. He had money—lots of it—and, in no uncertain terms, made it his mission to feed the masses. When this guy won, I'm telling you that his tips may very well have exceeded our salaries.

What could a writer/researcher position at an auction company possibly offer to contend with a near-perfect schedule and unsolicited supplemental income at the racetrack?

I recalled the details of my interview and tour of the warehouse. Casual attire was one (huge) plus. I would be writing catalog descriptions for auction items. These included bats and uniforms used by Major League players, autographed baseballs, and various other collectibles. Basically, I was to be paid to report to a building and handle a jersey worn by Brooks Robinson, a bat used by Eddie Murray, and a sideline jacket worn at Memorial Stadium by a former Colts player.

I had to take this position.

I surprised myself in that I really didn't give the matter much consideration. It turned out to be an excellent move. The things I physically touched and was assigned to describe were, as advertised, priceless heirlooms. A uniform worn by Babe Ruth on the 1935 U.S. Tour of Japan went for more than $750,000. There were several Ruth-wielded bats, some lumber employed by the likes of Gehrig, Foxx, and Cobb. There was a bra worn by one Britney Spears. It was as if I was five years old and had to go to Toys "R" Us five days a week.

Meanwhile, the offtrack facility was closed for a day by the Illinois Racing Board for a conflict of interest issue. The owners of the bar/restaurant on the site were paying off on the video poker machines and didn't heed the Racing Board's warning.

Two months later, the Romeoville Off-Track Betting facility was closed. For good.

64

Decoration by decoration, I have made my statement as loudly as I could. The six retired Orioles uniform numbers (20, 5, 22, 4, 33, and 8) are tattooed in orange-on-black block-style numerals on my left calf. Just to the left of that telling declaration, a tattoo of the Baltimore City flag only accents my stance.

I've had support, too. While chewing on a Now and Later (which, by the way, should have come with handwritten dentist recommendations) one night in Plainfield, Illinois, a crown on one of my back teeth came loose. My dentist fitted me for a replacement which, unbeknownst to me, had an Oriole bird painted on it. Dr. Todd Martin gets all of the credit for that one. He thought of it, not me. I think tooth adornments are about as far as you can go.

Credit Martin with having the foresight to know that his patient wouldn't object.

65

I attended a late-September Orioles-Tigers game at Camden Yards in 2004. We won, but in hindsight, all I can recall is the fact that the Tigers were absolutely dreadful and, two years later, were to reach the World Series while we continued to look for answers. There's nothing wrong with looking for answers, but when the good days become less and less frequent, it's extremely difficult to cope with surprising turnarounds as they transpire elsewhere.

I can offer no better example of this than what played out in 2004.

Natural rivals by virtue of their geographical location, the Boston Red Sox have had a history flecked with near misses, chokes, and torment that have long been blamed on a man who has been dead and buried since August 16, 1948. Is there such a thing as a "curse"? Well, when it's attributed to a Baltimore-born soul, I like to think so.

Fast-forward to the 2004 ALCS in which the Red Sox became the first-ever team to erase a three-games-to-none deficit and win a postseason series. Before this BoSox feat, no team had even come back to force a Game 7, much less win one. The World Series was, of course, anticlimactic.

The birth of Red Sox Nation.

I cannot think of any fan base more despicable than that of the Red Sox. Before you cite an earlier passage in which I announced a similar stance regarding Yankees fans, let me explain the difference: Yankee fans, rude; Red Sox fans, bandwagon. Five years after that long-awaited World Series conquest, they're still coming out of the woodwork under the guise of having been lifelong fans. To top it off, the motion picture *Fever Pitch* was a simultaneous box office smash, and now everybody climbs aboard.

What a mindless flock of sheep.

You guys were tortured (actually, your parents, grandparents, and great-grandparents were) for almost ninety years; and you finally won another championship. I get it. Now will you try to be slightly less obnoxious?

I'll tell you what, if I'm a Boston native, you're damn right I'm going to ride this thing all I can. But there are motherfuckers from Hyannis to Saudi Arabia jumping on the bandwagon, and it's nauseating.

Shortly after the New Year (2005), I flew to Baltimore to see a Loyola College-Canisius men's hoops game. I found a bar in Fell's Point called "One-Eyed Mike's." I walked into this place—walking distance from Camden Yards, mind you—and saw a huge Red Sox flag (I mean *huge*) hanging in the window. I asked the owner/bartender if this had become a Red Sox bar. He smugly replied, "Yeah, I guess you could say this *is* a Red Sox bar."

What a hollow prick. Absolute zero in the character department. I mean, truthfully, you can back who you damn well please; but if you examine the entire picture and the timely circumstances, what does this guy stand for? Does *he* even know?

I wouldn't go back into that shithole even if Beyoncé was giving free lap dances.

66

Some lessons are readily comprehended; others, not so much.

By the time the dust cleared on the 2005 Major League season and postseason, harsh realities had begun to sink in.

It's incredibly easy to look at a project four years later and recognize that the new building blocks didn't fit.

All of the sudden, I'm looking at a roster with Miguel Tejada in place and both Rafael Palmeiro and Sammy Sosa about to don the orange and black. Here are three superlock first-ballot Hall of Famers. Baltimore, you have a ball club. Again. Finally.

Through the first two and a half months, we were making sure we saved vacation time for October. Simultaneously, the Chicago White Sox were leading a charge of their own. The talk on the airwaves and on the printed page had the "experts" opining on just when both teams would come crashing back to earth. The White Sox actually had a record stretch in which they had enjoyed a lead in every single game of the season. Erik Bedard and the Orioles brought that to a halt with a win on a chilly Sunday afternoon in mid-May.

By mid-June, the Birds had been grounded. I drove out to Cincinnati for a Saturday night O's-Reds Interleague game. Cincinnati may very well be the filthiest and most depressing city I've ever encountered. The 10-1 Orioles loss didn't help. Sal Fasano's solo home run was the only thing that appealed to me from the moment I left my driveway in Lemont until the moment I fell asleep back home in Lemont early the next morning. As I exited the ballpark in Cincy, I couldn't imagine waking up in that city, so I drove back home and made it in time for last call—with the sinking foreboding that things weren't going to get much better.

When in a predicament, I've learned that an active role in bettering a situation is the only route. I've also learned never, ever, ever to tell myself that things can't get any worse.

They can, and they usually do.

Less than sixty days after standing all alone atop baseball's toughest division, the 2005 Orioles were under .500, fired their manager, and watched as Palmeiro was suspended for steroid use.

During the spiraling decline, I did make a flight to Baltimore for a Saturday afternoon Orioles-Indians game. At that time, the O's scheduled their Saturday games for 4:05 p.m. On this particular Saturday, I flew out in the morning and flew back the same night, sparing myself the hotel expense. My hero, Daniel Cabrera, blanked the Tribe that afternoon.

But even this triumph was not without its drawback.

Midway through the game, I watched from my vantage point along the first base line. Jay Gibbons absolutely scorched a foul ball that, I swear to you, made an audible whiz as it approached and passed by the area in which I was located. A distinctive *smack* interrupted the sphere's flight. It was the kind of sound that left listeners with the conclusion that the ball had most definitely hit a seat. Nothing else could have possibly produced this sound.

Moments later, I watched as paramedics were summoned to a location just three rows in front of my own seat. There, a middle-aged woman was doubled over, hands on face.

A pair of paramedics arrived and quickly lifted her to carry her up the rows. There was blood everywhere. Everywhere. As they began to make their way up the steps, the woman lost consciousness, and her arm dropped to her side, releasing the towel she had been holding to the spot of contact. There was a large black circle in the middle of her face. It appeared as though her nose was gone.

Just a black circle in its place.

It was a very disturbing scene and an equally disturbing chapter in Orioles history.

67

Back in Chicago that same summer, I attended a White Sox-Angels weekday matinee. For the record, let it be noted that my friend Tony Baranek of Chicago *Daily Southtown* fame provided me with a ticket. It was basically an afternoon excursion with myself, Tony, and some area high school sports coaches. A fun outing, to be sure. I only clarify these details for fear of planting the thought that I would attend a random White Sox game during a time that throngs of Chicagoans were jumping on the bandwagon. I had no such purpose.

I was driving home one afternoon during the late 1980s and saw a parking spot less than a block away from Wrigley Field. For this stroke of fate, nothing more, I took the spot, walked across the street, and bought a ticket to a Cubs-Phillies game. I think Von Hayes hit a couple of homers that day. There was one other game, a regular season finale between the Cubs and Pirates, and I think it was 1988. I walked down to that one (it was freezing that day) only because I preferred even the most meaningless of baseball games to the company at our apartment that day.

I'm really not entertained by non-Orioles baseball. The players, stadiums, uniforms, and fan customs just don't appeal to me. There's never really a reason for me to attend. So unless a rock-star parking spot appears, or an opportunity to escape the nonsensical rant of Tuna Carey presents itself, or a chance to sit in the sun with my boss and our favorite high school sports mentors arises, you won't find me at a game that doesn't involve the Orioles.

So there I am in a circus-like setting whose electricity I can only hope will quickly fade—as it had in every other season. I can tell you year after year that I despise the White Sox. And I do. But the fascinating aspect of this ongoing hatred is that there is never a chance that its intensity will ease up. They give me new reasons to hate them every time I'm in that despicable ballpark. This 2005 afternoon was no exception.

Where else but U.S. Cellular Field would I witness a clinic on fair-weather fans?

Local "hero" Frank Thomas (who, mind you, did nothing but produce during his entire career in Chicago, yet was the subject of criticism all the while) made his season debut that day, prompting "heartfelt" cheers with his every plate appearance.

Late in the game with the Angels leading, Timo Perez was announced as a pinch hitter for Thomas. Unbeknownst to the fans in attendance, Thomas had been lifted as a precautionary measure, not a strategic one. Perez, of course, had an uneventful at-bat; and the crowd booed vociferously. If ever I witnessed the entire gathering turn on a player—as if to demand his head—it was after Perez had failed in this particular pinch-hitting role.

About an hour later, Angels closer Francisco Rodriguez was on the ropes, facing Perez with two outs in the bottom of the ninth with the potential tying run at third and the would-be winning run on second. Perez lined a walk-off single, and the scene that followed cemented the White Sox fans as the most fickle I will ever see.

As the crowd exited down the ramps, the White Sox "fans" chanted in unison: "Tee-Mo! Tee-Mo!"

Yes, the same "Tee-Mo" whose ears, nose, and dick they would have ceremoniously chopped off only an hour earlier.

I cannot tolerate people like that.

*They're writing songs of love,
But not for me.*

—Ira Gershwin

68

It's impossible to accurately define the Orioles' 2005 collapse merely by chronicling it. The lone analogy that comes to mind is one of a prizefighter. This pugilist is getting pummeled. He is the recipient of repeated blows—a flurry of jabs, uppercuts, and left and right crosses.

But the bell never rings.

I returned to Baltimore in August of 2005; the hosts' swoon in full swing. I watched as the Red Sox administered a sound beating. I was surrounded by Bostonians, a foreigner in my own beloved ballpark.

All I could hope for at this juncture was that the White Sox would be caught. They damn near collapsed, but in the end, Cleveland had simply dug itself a hole it could not quite escape. I could only look on in horror and listen to cries of "He gone!" from Hawk Harrelson.

There are few, if any, announcers whose combination of thorough baseball knowledge and storytelling abilities rival those of Harrelson. But he loses me when he bitches about every call that doesn't go Chicago's way and yet will never admit when his team gets a break. And the "He gone!" shit is taunting. If you're not going to say it for batters from both teams, then it's clear to me that your sole intention is to piss people off.

The lesson I learned that fall was a simple one: I should mind my own business. My worst nightmare was unfolding. I was surrounded by White Sox fans claiming lifelong allegiance. I absolutely did *not* want this team to win. Every bar I went to, people talked about how long they've been waiting for this, spinning yarns that they had attended upward of thirty games a year for the last ten seasons. Really? The attendance figures say otherwise—unless I happened to have the grave and coincidental misfortune of somehow meeting all nine thousand of the people who *have* been attending for the last ten years. They got on my last nerve. They knew how to press my buttons, and like an idiot, I let them aggravate me.

We'll never know how many NBA games were decided because of referees who had sizable wagers on games that they worked. We'll never know how many bullshit holding or pass interference calls (and non-calls) were intentionally levied so as to sway the course of NFL contests. And we'll never know how many Major League umpires had a financial interest in the games in which they served as arbiters.

The 2005 ALCS still has me wondering about the latter possibility.

The dropped third strike call that altered the course of Game 2 ranks among the most horrific rulings I've even seen. The non-call of catcher's interference in Game 3 ranks right up there, too.

I doubt it will ever be proven, but for whatever reason, the umpires seemed hell-bent on a White Sox world championship in 2005.

It infuriated me what that team got away with, and it infuriated me even more that these simpletons actually believed that they won it fair and square.

Right. And OJ didn't butcher Nicole and Ron.

69

Nothing is sure to draw your ire more than having someone try to "correct" a wrong that isn't wrong to begin with.

A few years back, I had a neon Oriole bird custom made. It was the cartoon bird that appeared on the caps from 1966 through 1988 (you know the one, the cute little guy from back when we ruled the baseball world). I hung it in my third-story window; and as my condo building was on a hill to begin with, whenever I lit it, you could literally see it from more than a mile away. As folks exited from I-55 and drove over the bridge on Lemont Road, the bird, when lit, was a telltale sign that the Orioles had prevailed that day/night. After more than two seasons of lighting my bird to proclaim triumph (which hadn't been too often), I received a knock on my door one night.

It was the newly elected condo association board president. A thankless position that, in this unfortunate incidence, had been taken over by a middle-aged bitch on a power trip. She ordered me to remove the bird from the window, citing bylaw No. 438-A (or something like that), which stated that all window dressings must be approved by fellow residents.

Enraged, I told her that I had the bird on display (during baseball season only) for more than two years, and nobody seemed to mind.

"Well, they're complaining now," was her completely concocted reply.

I then inquired about the unit owner on the second floor who had a White Sox pennant in his window. Why was that okay but my bird wasn't?

Do you know what this twisted shrew did? She went down to the guy's unit and told him that I filed a complaint regarding his White Sox pennant. She didn't cite the same "iron rules" for him, she simply blamed it on me.

So I made an adjustment. I hung the bird in the back of my unit, and now when I lit it up, the neon would reflect off the large glass frames that hung all over my sacred black walls. This bird was now readily visible from the same distances and at far more angles than it had been. Trumping that maneuver was my Christmas display that December. During that joyous season, of course, bylaws went, well, out the window (pardon the jest). Throughout my building, red-and-green lights were strewn about every last windowsill with accents such as "Merry Christmas," "Peace," and "Joy" by people who truly believe that their meager Sunday contributions into the wicker basket are going to thwart inevitable nothingness or, worse yet, eternal damnation for an existence based largely on hypocrisy.

I purchased lights, as well. But I arranged them in my windows to read "52" in tribute to Ravens linebacker Ray Lewis. Surely, they couldn't protest my decorative statement. Not with the collective electric show they were simultaneously running.

Miss President's daughter approached me in Tom's Place one night, feeling no pain, and asked what the numbers represented.

"Ray Lewis," I replied. "He's the coolest."

"You're an asshole," she shouted back and walked away.

That was actually what I wanted to hear.

70

The ebb and flow of a franchise's fortunes will, over time, tax one's patience. Add to that your reactions to attitudes and behavior that are as much a part of the game as the seventh-inning stretch, and it will drive you right up a fucking wall.

If you let it.

The simple truth is that faith, a complete lack of faith, and transparent insincerity are all universal. These traits are just more simple to recognize in sports. The whole Red Sox Nation concept represents a charade of colossal proportions. It does to me, anyway. I recall watching 2008 NBA Finals footage on SportsCenter. There at courtside in Boston was a group of Red Sox players that included Curt Schilling. These guys appeared as though they really belonged there. The immediate question that came to mind, however, was where the fuck were they just one year prior, pre-Garnett, when the Celtics were the NBA doormat? I'll tell you where they were: somewhere else. Don't kid yourself about pride and support. If those Red Sox players knew anything about either of those elements, they'd have been courtside the year before, too. And the year before that, too.

"Your team" is an overnight powerhouse, and you're going to seize every photo opportunity to show what a faithful comrade you are. I get it. I just define loyalty a little differently.

And as much as the flocks converge as soon as a team starts winning, the converse holds true.

It's absolutely tragic that Red Sox and Yankee fans outnumber the locals when their teams come to Camden Yards. But the bottom line is that the right to an available ticket to a baseball game, no matter where it's played, is theirs. The operative word, of course, is "available." Blame is to go to Baltimoreans for allowing this. These are the same people who screamed bloody murder when the Colts were whisked out of town in the middle of the night. The same people that left thousands of Memorial Stadium seats empty when "their team" struggled throughout the 1983 season.

I walked into Mick O'Shea's on a recent visit to Baltimore, wearing a T-shirt with the 1970s cartoon bird logo on the front. Someone approached and declared, "That's what we need, not this current bird, but the cartoon one. We used to *win* when we had *that* bird."

I've got news for you, pal, we don't need a new logo. We need believers on the field and in the stands. Am I the only one that's sickened when walking down Howard Street, directly across from Camden Yards, to witness vendors displaying Red Sox and Yankees shirts and hats for sale? Is it really all about catering to these people and making a dollar? Is there any way to police these vendors, or is it a matter of free enterprise? Because I'd be considerably less offended to see a stand hawking hardcore porn or a display with "I Love Hitler" T-shirts and serial-killer keepsakes paying homage to Speck, Gacy, Dahmer—you know, all the greats.

This isn't about winning and losing. This is about civic pride. I chose long ago to embrace Baltimore, and I'm going to support its combatants in their every effort.

I draw an analogy to parenthood. What if your child earned straight A's all through grade school but had trouble adjusting to high school (like so many of us have) and slipped to C's and D's? Would you abandon the kid? Or better yet, would you set out to adopt a neighbor's kid who *was* getting those straight A's?

When explained in those terms, it sounds ridiculous. But that's exactly the mind-set of so many "fans" today.

Your struggles and triumphs are your own, and either adjustments or celebrations should be made accordingly. I recently saw highlights of a Big Ten hoops game between Illinois and host Penn State. Displayed in sizable lettering along the base line was NITTANY NATION.

Is originality really that difficult? Are identities limited only to those that are all the rage?

It's a sad state of affairs in Baltimore when the Red Sox are in town and their fans take over our beautiful stadium. And that's on Baltimore citizens, who should support their Orioles regardless of status. It's your team.

And I'll be the first to admit that it is completely the right of Red Sox fans to buy as many available tickets as they desire. It's also *my* right to not hold the door for them when they're walking behind me. It's my right, as well, to sit on a jam-packed Light Rail car and leave a mother (in a Red Sox jersey) standing with a baby in her arms.

I know how that kid is going to grow up: as a sheep following the crowd.

Success does not automatically warrant respect. I believe it to be very sad that so many people cannot think and act on their own. So many are unable to resist joining the most plentiful of flocks as if they were obligated in some way.

If access to the Boston Celtics locker room is what it requires to be "cool," I'll have to take a pass.

You can give my ticket to Michael Phelps. I think he might enjoy that.

If you're going through hell, keep going.

—Winston Churchill

71

Attempting as I have, without achievement, to move to Baltimore, my efforts have seemed halfhearted in retrospect. With repeated failure, that's the logical view in a results-oriented culture. Truthfully though, I have made concerted efforts, even strides that had me believing—for one or two rapturous seconds—that I had finally made it.

Year after year, the miles have piled up. A twenty-five-minute drive to Midway Airport and a weekend sojourn in Baltimore—rarely causing me to miss any workdays. Four times in 2004. Five trips in 2005 (plus four O's games at U.S. Cellular and another in Cincinnati). Six flights in 2006. Seven times in 2007. Seven more in 2008. While trips of this frequency obviously haven't been enough to sate me, they've been a steadily increasing sign to family and friends that I have a destination in mind.

There have been other visits, too. A Chris Rock stand-up concert at the Lyric lured me. So did Goodwill of the Chesapeake, for which I annually volunteered on Thanksgiving at the Baltimore Convention Center, flew out there and served food to the city's less fortunate each year from 2003 through 2007. I hesitate to tell of the latter journeys for fear of sounding like a do-gooder inclined to pat himself on the back. I want to clear that notion by saying that like every other trip to Baltimore, the Thanksgiving trips were self-serving. Three or four hours wearing an apron followed by a night of festivities in Fell's Point. I did my part in the soup kitchen, yes, but I'm not sure that I really helped. I'm not sure any of us did. In the big picture, those people are either back on the street or sitting in a bar playing Keno the next day.

Make no mistake. I go to Baltimore to soak up a culture and have as much fun as I can. In that regard, I'm very selfish.

As well received as my pilgrimages may have been by the suits at Goodwill, my repeated inquiries regarding employment opportunities were not. Nor did I impress the Maryland Food Bank.

But even in repeated disappointment, I've learned that perhaps my wealth lies in my faithful friends, certainly not in my marketable traits. Old Towson friends, Regan and Lisa, each did their part in landing me an interview, going out of their way to do so. Neither of those job quests came to fruition, nor did a later possibility with the Maryland Multi-Housing Association, an opportunity arranged by perhaps my most helpful and true friend, Cindy, another Towson University cohort.

Then there were "opportunities" created by my own hunting. An announcement of a job fair brought me to Towson. Contrary to the details in an online description, this was not a "job" fair, but rather, an "internship" fair. And that's fine—actually worthwhile—if you're a nineteen-year-old student in search of experience and contacts. But for a middle-aged Orioles fanatic, the whole thing serves no purpose other than to be an excuse to maybe attend a college basketball game and find a watering hole at his old college campus.

In January 2006, an Internet effort got me in the door at the Greater Baltimore Medical Center. I flew out and flew back to Chicago that same night, feeling confident about my performance during the interview.

And nothing. Not even the phone call they had promised I'd get "either way." Oh, who am I kidding. I was crushed long before I realized that my phone was never going to ring. The day after my interview at GBMC, the 13-3 Ravens held Indianapolis to zero touchdowns in an AFC play-off game—and still lost, 15-6. That's what I think of every time I'm reminded of GBMC, not the fact that they never called like they promised they would.

I harbor no animosity and make no complaints, though. Not just because of my firm belief that Baltimore establishments can do no wrong, but because in retrospect, I was not suited for any of those positions. These potential employers plainly recognized that. Square pegs will not fit into round holes.

Err I give up.

72

Labels drive me crazy. How 'bout you? What really irks me is when one stupid incident causes people to rave about someone for the rest of his career. I guess you can liken it to the halo effect.

I needn't look beyond Kevin Millar for a definitive example of this phenomenon. Here's a mediocre (at best) player who was in the right place at the right time. The 2004 Red Sox are down three-games-to-none to the Yankees, and Millar says it's time to "cowboy up."

Well, well, what do you know? A miracle happens, the Red Sox win, and Kevin Millar is now a "great clubhouse guy." Really? Was he a great "clubhouse guy" during his subsequent tenure with the Orioles? Did he help us win? By the way, what exactly does a good "clubhouse guy" do to help a team win? Does he lead by example? Well, if that's the criteria for a good "clubhouse guy," Kevin Millar does *not* fit that billing.

People make shit up all the time. In my own family, I'm guessing there are more people who make stuff up (and believe it) than there are people who are honest. There are tales that have very little foundation, but they just keep growing with one fictitious addition after another. The label sticks to whomever they're referring, unfortunately; and as is the case with Millar, it's a bell that cannot be unrung.

The night before Manny Ramirez hit career home run No. 500 in Baltimore, the tone for the entire series (a series in which the Orioles were swept) was set—by Millar.

In the bottom of the twelfth in a 2-2 game, Nick Markakis doubled with one out. Aubrey Huff then drew a walk, and Millar came to the plate. He hit a soft grounder to late-inning replacement Julio Lugo, who let the ball play him and resultantly bobbled it. As Millar *jogged* down the first base line, Lugo hurried and fired to first to get the out. If Millar shows even the slightest morsel of hustle, the bases are loaded with one out and red-hot Luke Scott is coming to the plate. Instead, Scott was walked intentionally to load the bases, Ramon Hernandez flied out, and the inning was over. Boston tallied three times in the top of the thirteenth, and every semblance of life was completely sucked out of the Orioles.

That is what I'll always remember about Kevin Millar. That and a bunch of line drive foul balls.

What, by the way, is the literal translation for "cowboy up?" Is that what you're doing when you decide it's not important to hustle in the bottom of the twelfth inning?

Beats me.

73

Certain passages refuse to leave even the most remote compartments of my memory. Some of them, well, I'm not sure why I can't forget them. Like the one I heard on September 9, 1981. On a school night at sixteen, I was up (as usual) past a reasonable hour. On the *Tomorrow* show, host Tom Snyder announced that it was "square root day." Nine times nine equals eighty-one. That's kind of cool. Doesn't happen very often, either.

A more poignant message has stuck with equal potency. It's a line in Woody Allen's *Manhattan*. Near the end of the film, Tracy (Mariel Hemingway) is literally on her way to the airport to make an overseas journey. Initially, she had balked at the idea, believing it would perhaps sever the ties between her and Woody Allen (who was about thirty years her senior). Allen, entangled in more age-appropriate affairs, urged her to seize it as a wonderful opportunity.

Given time to think, Allen is suddenly belted with the realization that this is a sweet and beautiful girl, one he should appreciate for as long as he is able. He rushes (on foot) to Tracy's apartment, only to find her waiting in the lobby for a taxicab to begin her lengthy journey. Allen pleads with her not to go—a complete contradiction to his stance just a few days ago. It is at this moment we realize that Tracy intends to stay true, telling Allen "You have to have a little faith in people."

That sentiment never goes out of style. And it applies to personal relationships on every level, not just those of the romantic variety. Until you're willing to make even a token effort to learn about someone, you'll be in the dark, convinced that your prejudices hold water. And they don't, not as a blanket assumption.

*It was never clear what would come next,
But that's the risk and that's the test.*

—Shawn Colvin

74

I've come to realize that, if nothing else, I will always have Baltimore—at a distance. I never worry about myself. I'm old enough to know what's right. I'm not very talented in any specific activity, actually. But I have one thing for which I'm thankful: the ability to choose correctly without having experienced what's behind the door I just chose. I'm not very good in conversation. In fact, I usually don't engage in them. I can put my thoughts on paper with some degree of eloquence, but they seldom come out of my mouth with the same effect.

I was aware of my innate ability to wisely embrace or ignore something at an early age. I knew from the first time I looked at spinach that it would be revolting. Have I ever tried it? No, but I still know that it would taste like shit.

So as I continue to come to Baltimore, I grow less and less a stranger in a strange town. One by one, block by block, everything I touch is wonderful. But this brings no grand elation and doesn't prompt me to share my new discoveries with the folks back home. The unassuming acceptance of Baltimore's wondrous traits mirrors Baltimore itself. There are no surprises. I knew it was perfect before I got here.

Every time.

Nobody I've ever known will be impressed when I tell them what happened to me in Baltimore. So I don't bother to share those tales. It's not that they wouldn't be happy for me realizing what some much-maligned East Coast city has done for my well-being. It's just that the same things wouldn't excite them.

I am obliged to be thankful (and I am) that I can recognize the simplest of joys and be content seeking only those ironclad truths. Visit by visit, I've come to the point of recognizing faces on the streets of Baltimore—no small feat for someone whose permanent residence is more than seven hundred miles to the west. I could go home to comfortable living quarters with an easily affordable mortgage. Gainful employment, as well. And for the past eight years, I've done that.

But not before leaving pieces of my soul at various spots in Baltimore. And I am wiser for having done so.

I cannot cite a precise calendar date; but somewhere along the way, I left Illinois, my family, my childhood acquaintances, schools, parks, and neighborhoods. I left it for good. Maybe I was never a part of those elements. Supplanting those things were ideas and people—almost exclusively conceived or met in Baltimore.

Give me Charles Street. There, I can walk southward and step on rose petals near the entrance of Ixia. I won't consider Chicago's Michigan Avenue or the Magnificent Mile as Charles Street's equivalent because, well, now I only have one street. I only have one of everything now.

Travel, discover, learn. I suggest everybody do these things. You'll experience great things you wouldn't have ordinarily encountered. Baltimore is my destination. There, not only do I have the Orioles, but I also have the Ravens, and I have Peabody. I'm no critic, but as cellists go, Zane Baker is without peer.

The Club Charles remains, as if it had waited for me since 1987, the same neon signs and decorations, unaltered.

I'm right about a lot of things. Things that nobody ever bothers to point out.

Any adult who wears the same clothes on successive days is seriously troubled. I have no use for them.

A seat belt on an airplane has never prevented injury or death.

Jim Palmer was the greatest pitcher to ever take the mound.

It is physically impossible to fall asleep on an airplane. I know I sure can't do it.

Never say always.

Never say never—unless you are talking about the possibility of someday spotting a homeless Japanese person begging for money with a tin cup.

For my $5 ticket offering, Siobhan Prior is the best bargain I've ever watched. The most talented player on the college women's hoops circuit? Hardly. But she has a heart too big for her body.

The angled center field warning track at Houston's Minute Maid Park is a career-ending injury waiting to happen, like the neighborhood pit bull that everyone fears but won't be put down until *after* it attacks and harms/kills a neighborhood kid. When it's too late.

*M*A*S*H** was the most unfunny television show I ever forced myself to sit through. Didn't understand the fanfare. Still don't.

Amber over Anita (this one is a no-brainer).

How do third-base umpires occasionally rule that a runner left too early when attempting to score on a sacrifice fly? Do they have the unique ability to focus on the baserunner's foot with one eye and the ball going into the outfielder's glove with the other—simultaneously?

Give. As much as you can. Someday, somewhere, it all comes back to you; and along the way, you'll restore the faith that so many of us lack.

The benches in Baltimore that proclaim "Baltimore—The Greatest City in America" are entirely accurate.

There are *way* more trees in this world than there are people. Way more.

I view Major League Baseball players the same way I did at the age of ten—as my elders.

While I'm quite firm on these statements, I'm aware that they are subject to debate. The one belief for which I will not listen to contrary views, however, is my assessment of Baltimore as the place I was supposed to be for the entirety of my existence.

About two months into the 2008 season, right around Interleague time, I instinctively found an auction house in Maryland. Actually, I found it on the Internet and mailed my resume.

Keeping with my fruitless track record—nothing.

I followed up with a telephone call and again, nothing.

And then, as if God himself had picked up a telephone and dialed my number accidentally, my phone rang. I was in my car en route to work at Mastro's Burr Ridge, Illinois warehouse. It was the head writer at Huggins & Scott, the Maryland auction house to which I had applied. I actually remembered the guy from a brief stint he had at Mastro a couple of years prior. I remembered that he was a Phillies fan, and I remembered that he had been a schoolteacher at one point. Bonus points for my retention capacity.

We scheduled an interview for early September as I already had a plane ticket to Baltimore to see the Orioles-Twins series.

More than a month passed between our telephone conversation and my face-to-face interview, but as I anticipated the opportunity, I was confident. It was obviously a position for which I was suited.

Simultaneously, the shit hit the fan at Mastro Auctions. A well-publicized FBI probe was underway, accusations and rumors were prevalent, and here I am about to board a plane to see if I could jump ship.

I'm sure that's how it seemed to my fellow employees, but nothing was further from the truth. I had been treated better at Mastro Auctions than I had been at any other job. Everyone at Mastro (save for one photographer) was solid gold. I wasn't trying to leave over concern for what might lie ahead, for what might go down in the wake of these investigations. I had expressed my interest in the Maryland-based competitor months before any of Mastro's woes had surfaced.

I made apartment-hunting appointments, I dusted off my (only) suit, and I got ready.

This one just *had* to work.

*And I won't forget to send you a card with my regrets
'cause I'm never gonna come back home.*

—Mary Chapin Carpenter

75

On the night before I flew out for my interview, I took every possible precautionary measure. I was not going to miss this flight. I set two separate alarm clocks and even set the alarm on my cell phone. Early to bed, early to rise.

The plan was working without flaw until Matt Phelan sent me repeated text messages at around 2:00 a.m. The T-Mobile alerts woke me up, and I wasn't going to fall back asleep. I knew this.

As I lay there, wide fucking awake, well past 3:00 a.m., another text message. This one, unexpectedly, was from a local bartender about two blocks away. "You awake?" she asked. I responded, "Yes, I am now."

I got absolutely zero sleep after those text alerts. So all told, I got about three solid hours. It would have to be enough. It would have to.

I got out of bed, pretty alert, showered, dressed, and got to Midway Airport without incident. My flight went without incident, too. So did my trip to Huggins & Scott in downtown Silver Spring.

I toured the office, met the relatively few employees on hand, sat down with the company suits (only one of whom was wearing a suit) and talked about the industry and the opportunity at hand. Salary? I gave them a figure.

"When can you start?" asked Bill Huggins, who is actually distant kin to Murderers Row manager Miller Huggins.

I had a job. A virtual ticket to move to Baltimore, Maryland, and stay there for the rest of my life. Sixteen percent pay cut, thirty-two miles to and from work, no health insurance, and as it turned out, a tiny $700-per-month studio apartment in place of my one-bedroom loft with a mortgage payment of $437.16.

Did I make out, or did I make out?

The greatest single day nonpareil.

I returned the rental car, went back to BWI, and waited to board the Light Rail bound for downtown Baltimore to hunt for apartments. I noticed a young girl, probably in her twenties, sitting Indian style on the cement and studiously composing text messages on her cell phone. Cute. A unique look. A series of faint blemishes on her face, but the absolute deepest brown eyes I'd ever seen. As the train arrived, she approached me and made a waving motion. She was wearing a brown sweatshirt that read GALLAUDET in powder blue characters. She was deaf, and as I was to learn shortly thereafter, Gallaudet is a school for the deaf based in Washington, D.C.

As I stopped to comply with her motions, she held her cell phone out for me to see. A text message she had typed read: "Does this train go to Penn Station?" I looked at her and nodded affirmatively. She responded in like fashion.

We boarded the same car and sat adjacent to one another. Shortly into the ride, I entered a text on my phone and showed her:

"Are you an Orioles fan?"

She read it and shrugged her shoulders as if to convey "sort of."

A few years ago, at the Main Inn in downtown Lemont, Illinois, I learned how to make a shirt out of U.S. paper currency. Quickly, as my stop was fast approaching and this girl was to stay aboard before reaching her own destination, I made one, a nice one, out of a one-dollar bill.

The train reached my stop, and I stood up and handed the origami creation to my new acquaintance. She held it, admired it, and as I turned to get off the train, she blew me a kiss and smiled.

It was the most genuine smile I had ever seen.